Five Secrets of Million Dollar Producers

A guide to killing it in the commercial insurance industry

By Monica M. Minkel, RPLU, MLIS

First Emerging Risks paperback edition 2016.

Minkel, Monica M.,
Five Secrets of Million Dollar Producers
1.   Business & Money / Insurance / Liability
2.   Business & Finance / Sales
3.   Marketing & Sales / Sales & Selling
ISBN-13: 978-1530643592
ISBN-10: 1530643597
ASIN B01NCLHA7L

For all the account managers in the insurance industry.

You are the heroes in this business.

Thank you for the support.

Table of Contents

Introduction

My insurance career started like most: completely by accident. In high school, I worked a variety of customer service related jobs like food service and retail. When I was in college, I decided I wanted to work where the money was and that meant a bank. I worked in banking for several years, doing every job from part-time drive through teller up to running the teller line and assisting with the management of the branch. I was working in the commercial loan department when I received a call from one of the largest insurance companies in the world, AIG. Initially skeptical, I asked for the location of the office and conveniently had an interview at a bank nearby the following week. I agreed to take the interview with AIG simply because they could see me immediately after my bank interview. That's all it took. After a great interview, I was offered the insurance company job. I took it and happily, I can say that I never looked back.

Insurance is a funny industry; quirky would be another word for it. Very few of my peers and counterparts set out to be insurance employees of any type. Many of us found our roles because we had a customer service background, a finance background or a sales background. Business insurance attracts a wide range of skills, backgrounds, and abilities. Compared to many other industries, insurance is a relatively stable career path. It is recession resistant in some ways because companies need insurance regardless of the underlying economic factors of the economy. The difference is that companies need more when they are growing and less when contracting. Premiums may fluctuate but the underlying need remains. While layoffs occur from time to time, often these are predicated by a merger or consolidation of two or more agencies. I also learned that there was more financial upside working in insurance than there had been at the bank and that certainly was an attractive characteristic.

While my insurance career started with an insurance company, often referred to as a carrier, I was quickly recruited to a customer facing role as a broker. The role of the broker is to represent the client/insurance buyer to the insurance company/carrier and negotiate for the best terms, conditions and pricing. The role has some challenges to determine customer needs and to match those needs up to the appropriate corresponding insurance product. The broker role is rewarding because you have a real opportunity to help protect a growing company from financial hardship or collapse. The proper procurement of insurance products can provide the needed safety net and security. A company needs insurance to protect its financial future when accidents and calamities happen. The hardest part about being a broker is that the customer is relying upon you to find a solution. If you can't find the solution for them, they will find someone else who can. While an underwriter may decline to write an account (and many underwriters regularly decline most of the opportunities presented to them), a broker is under much more pressure to find the right product or solution for the customer's needs. The broker cannot afford to be as selective when assessing whether to accept new customers. In many ways, the broker is the customer of the carrier. Conversely, the client is the customer of the broker.

Fortunately, I was recruited into a specialty area of insurance commonly referred to as Financial Services or Management

Liability. There are nine products that I focus on and I have developed an extensive depth of knowledge in this specific area. I say I was fortunate because I developed a lucrative specialty early in my career. As a product specialist, I found myself working with a wide range of sales Producers.

The Producers in the insurance brokerage market are the 'rain makers', the 'cold callers', the relationship managers. If the Producer doesn't sell, the agency does not win new accounts. The Producers are the ones making the calls, setting the first appointment and managing the overall relationship between the customer and the service team. In my role, I have worked with around 150 different Producers, some very experienced and talented and some very inexperienced and lacking sales skills of any kind. I have had the opportunity to go out on calls and meet clients with these producers. In this process, I have learned a lot about what works and what doesn't.

At this point in my career, I can tell if a new Producer is going to "make it" within about three meetings and often faster. I see the same mistakes over and over again. I watch insurance brokerage firms throw away large sums of money on Producers that don't stand a chance and couldn't sell property insurance to the owner of a building that was on fire. Insurance is something that every business owner needs. So why does a business owner choose one broker over another? What is a client really looking for when selecting their representation in the insurance marketplace?

The purpose of this book is to help aspiring insurance Producers avoid the most common mistakes and build that elusive million-dollar book of business. Successful Producers make my job easier and more fun. There is nothing more frustrating to a service team than to watch the associate Producers or developing Producers wash out year after year. There is a steep learning curve in the first year. The secrets outlined in this book will help you overcome the learning curve faster and avoid many of the common mistakes.

The success rate is atrocious for Producers new to the industry. Depending on the broker or agency, the new producer success rate can be as low as 30%. This means that 7 out of 10 fail in the first year. And the statistics show that another one or two will fail in year two. This is a tough business. It's not for everyone, not by a long shot. It's a big waste of money for the agency or brokerage firm to pay salaries for Producers who don't get past the first year. It is also incredibly difficult for a Producer to bounce from agency to agency and it's costly both in the opportunity cost and actual dollars.

Why do Producers fail? There are those who are simply bad hires from the beginning. There are people who come into this role not understanding the process or not having the very basic customer interaction skills. Frequently, the agency fails to provide adequate structure or sufficient accountability and without any specific direction, the producer flounders. Other times, the agency provides proper structure but the Producer does not connect with the right niche or network with the right people. A successful insurance Producer needs to be able to make cold calls, develop a network for referrals, and manage warm leads. But most of all, follow up and follow through strategies are paramount for success. The best lead network in the world will not pay off if the producer lacks follow up skills. If you sit in your office and wait for the phone to ring, you will be waiting a very long time.

As you consider whether being an insurance Producer is the right role for you, keep in mind that you will get out of it what you put into it. It's not much more complicated than that. There is a suite of skills that need to be developed. Even if these traits or skills are not inherent, with a little effort many otherwise marginal Producers can find themselves to be remarkably successful when they understand the process. Steven Covey says you must begin with the end in mind. If you take the time to understand the five secrets, there is no reason that you won't be successful. When you have a road map for success then you just need to start by taking that first step.

Thanks for taking the time to read my perspective and please be sure to leave a review on Amazon, Kindle or whatever service or device you are using to read.

Now get to selling!

The Insurance Industry

The modern insurance industry began in about 1688 when patrons in Edward Lloyd's London based coffee shop agreed to share a portion of the risk on each other's vessels (ships) in exchange for their peers accepting a portion of the risk on their own vessels. For example, when ten merchants and ship owners each agreed to accept 10% of the risk of loss on each of the ten ships in the group, everyone limited their exposure to a complete loss from a disaster that might sink their own ship. This risk sharing concept launched the modern insurance industry and in some ways, is still followed at the iconic Lloyds of London today. While the underlying function may be similar, the concept of risk sharing has evolved greatly since then.

In 2004, I had the amazing experience of visiting London and touring the Lloyds of London building with my favorite underwriters. I felt like a VIP on the tour as my host underwriters gave us the insider experience. We saw the bell, the amazing atrium, sat in a 'box' and so much more. It was a humbling experience to appreciate the concept of the queue and see how business was done long before the invention of email or even the telephone. We also visited the location of the original Lloyds coffee house where the modern insurance industry was established

There are three basic concepts to manage risk or uncertainty. Risk Avoidance is the complete removal of risk. In this concept, there is no participation in the activity or property. For example, you might choose to not fly on an airplane or not purchase a piece of property to avoid risk. The second concept is Risk Financing where you set aside the funds necessary to manage the risk if something goes wrong. For instance, you may purchase the item of property, but hold back enough money so that you could replace the property if it were damaged or destroyed. A Captive Insurance Company program would be an example of Risk Financing. The final concept is the idea of Risk Transfer or transferring some or all the risk to another party. With Risk Transfer, the property would be purchased but most the financial risk is transferred to another party where the loss would be primarily absorbed by the third party. The purchase of an insurance policy is an example of the concept of Risk Transfer.

In its simplest terms, the modern insurance marketplace serves to transfer the financial risk of loss from a company's own balance sheet to a third party using an insurance product. Insurance is often called a 'risk transfer' mechanism for this reason. Insurance allows companies to share risk among themselves by paying insurance premiums that are later used to pay out claims. Insurance premiums are aggregated among all the insured parties. This pooling of resources reduces the risk of any single company being forced to pay out a large loss from their own pocket.

The insurance industry encompasses a number of different products ranging from Workers Compensation and Property coverage to more recent creations such as Employment Practices Liability insurance and Cyber Liability insurance. Lloyds of London taught us that almost anything is insurable for the right price and under the right conditions. In my experience with one of the largest insurance companies in the world, this concept held true. In many instances, we looked at ways to offer our product to the customer while excluding the most obvious risks and setting the price at a level where we knew we could take a hit occasionally and the actuaries would still be happy with us. The broker's role is important in ensuring that the most important needs of the client are covered even when the underwriter seeks to limit exposure.

Insurance is constantly evolving. The products evolve, the carriers change, new players come in and others walk away or change their appetites. Those who enter a career in the insurance industry should maintain a lifelong interest in learning about coverage, markets, and exposures. The hunger for constant learning will be obvious to your clients and prospective clients. It is helpful to understand the history of many of the products and processes that we use. In addition, it is important to watch for emerging opportunities and changes that can impact client needs and the availability of coverage.

To be a successful producer, you must understand the product that you sell and the needs of your buyer. It seems as if many Producers fail to appreciate that a general understanding of business is not only important but incredibly relevant. If the Producer seeks to understand the challenges and triumphs of a business owner or executive, that Producer is far more likely to anticipate their needs and provide more accurate, thorough and customized solutions. Some of the most successful Producers have small business backgrounds themselves. When a Producer has experience as a business owner or executive, they better understand a business owner's needs and the way that decisions are made. The business owner perspective is incredibly valuable in the sales process. And even if you have not owned a business or been an executive, you can take some time to think about the needs inherent in those roles. When you approach your client with an understanding of their needs and perspective, you are far more likely to make a connection and offer a solution that solves a problem they are experiencing.

One of our Account Executives announced one day at a staff meeting that by spending an hour per week learning about a specific topic, you could be among the world's leading experts in less than ten years. The Account Executive further stated that if you can spend ten hours a week, you could be an expert in a year or less. Passion for insurance is less important than passion for business, problem solving, and customer service. The best Producers I know have an underlying drive to help others. If you start out seeking to understand the business needs of a client and ultimately their exposures, then you can seek to find the right insurance products to help manage and mitigate the risk. If you reverse the order of this concept and seek first to sell and then to figure out what they need, you will find yourself lacking in client growth. In addition, you may offer the wrong products or solutions and may miss out on opportunities because you get stuck trying to sell YOUR product not focusing on the client need.

Take some time to understand the different insurance products, what they do, what companies need them for and the nuances of coverage. You will not be an expert at everything, or even at most things. However, you can develop a very strong working understanding of coverage. This alone will help you avoid that "deer in the headlights" look when the conversation with a client or prospect takes an unexpected turn. Clients want to work with someone that knows at least as much as they do, preferably more. If you don't understand coverage basics, you will not be successful selling the products.

You can learn about insurance products by reading books and trade publications. National Underwriter is a popular and free magazine. Others include Property Casualty 360 and Business Insurance. Devote time each week to updating yourself on current trends and acquiring product knowledge. Your level of knowledge will help you cultivate a trusting relationship with your prospects. No one wants to buy something from someone that can't even explain how it works. Even though I am a specialist with only nine products in my department, I can explain the basics of General Liability, Workers Compensation and many other insurance policies. I'm not an expert at every line of coverage, but I understand enough of the basics to uncover needs and develop strategies to help the client. I also know how to engage the service teams for help.

There are a wide range of carriers with varying interests in different companies and products. Be sure you have a basic understanding of who writes what for whom. You will come across as more knowledgeable about the industry if you know that Chubb has an interest in contractors or that AIG stopped writing products for investment advisors. Again, curiosity about the industry and an understanding of the function and appetite of the carriers in the marketplace will help you build confidence with the clients you are serving.

Now that you have a very basic understanding of the industry and you are committed to learning all that you can, we can talk about the things that no one tells you when you become a Producer.

Shhhhhhhh......don't tell anyone.

What no one really tells you

"If you're offered a seat on a rocket ship, don't ask what seat!

Just get on." - Sheryl Sandberg

Ready to fail?

Would you take a job if I told you that there was a 70% chance you would be fired in the first year? The life cycle of an insurance producer can be quite volatile. Producers that are new to the industry have about a 70% failure rate in the first year. The failure rate is calculated on the expected (targeted) first year production as compared to actual production. Most new producers fall short of targeted production goals. In many companies, you have less than a year to prove yourself (even if you were told you have three years to 'ramp' or 'validate'). When your numbers aren't where they need to be, you get cut from the team. Often, new Producers know their production has not developed and they self-select themselves out of the organization (find another job and quit).

In my own experience, newly hired producers rarely see their first anniversary. This is a miserable statistic and one that is unfortunate both for the Producer and for the Company. A failed producer is a tremendous waste of money and time. Often the critical flaws are obvious from the first few days. I have worked with producers who simply found themselves in the wrong agency where their personality or strengths failed to match up well with the resources and overall goals of the organization itself. For other producers, it was an absence of intellectual curiosity, follow up skills, or basic business acumen that did them in. Regardless of the specific reason, the numbers are not in your favor.

Two examples:

- A Producer with a heavy restaurant background and connections in the food service industry joined an agency that had no significant restaurant clients, no restaurant specialists on the support staff and lacked market access to specific programs and underwriters dedicated to restaurants.
- A former personal lines captive agent joined a large national brokerage where the minimum account size was $10,000 or more. The relationships built with individuals and small businesses while the producer was a captive agent were completely wasted. Furthermore, the producer had always used a single product and quoted things directly and now they were working through an account management team to get things done. The absence of a follow up strategy was terminal.

Both producers failed.

Some estimates have the failure rate for new Producers as high as 92% or even 95%. Recently, an executive told me that their company's failure rate on new producers with no insurance background was 100% over a five-year period. 100%. That's insane! Many sales positions in other industries may have similar rates of turnover, yet most industries don't push the concept of the "Trusted Advisor" quite like the insurance industry does. How can we be developing trusted advisers for our clients if less than one in ten Producers will actually be around at the three or five-year mark?   There must be a better way.

'Validation' is a commonly used term that means the Producer has become profitable. Many agencies consider the producer profitable when production equals about 300% of the producer's base salary.   If the Producer is making a $50,000 salary, 'validation' occurs when $150,000 of recurring revenue is achieved. If the Producer is making a $100,000 salary, 'validation' occurs   once the Producer achieves $300,000 of recurring revenue. Some agencies use different terminology or metrics, but the concept is the same. Validation is effectively being able to pay for oneself without constantly facing the possibility of being terminated.

In a three-year period, I knew of a large regional agency that validated one producer out of nearly thirty.   The producer that validated learned Secret #2 and leveraged targeted relationships. This producer became laser focused on a single industry and built a large book of clients and a significant market share in this niche. Most often, producers are unable to translate their previous 'business experience' to the insurance sales role. When the real estate market crumbled, we picked up several sales professionals with heavy real estate backgrounds.   Every single one of these producers failed at our company. The real estate sale cycle and process is different from the insurance sales process. I don't know that anyone appreciated just how big of a leap these producers would have to make. Many of them went right back to real estate when the market recovered.

In the interview process, it is very unlikely that anyone disclosed the firm's wash out rate. Talking about failures is not the best way to attract new talent. The executives probably talked about their great training program, fantastic support staff and the amazing services the firm provides to its customers. What they likely didn't disclose was that they had not 'validated' or 'qualified' a new Producer in three years and the odds of becoming their next success story were very low. The ability to succeed at any firm is incumbent upon you and your ability to use the resources available to your advantage. All companies have some successful Producers and all have some failing Producers. What does it take to succeed in your firm? You will need to follow those steps to accomplish your production goals.

Many Producers start at one company and move on to the next, and the next, and the next. Moving from agency to agency is not the way to become a million-dollar Producer. In fact, it's the worst way to retain your clients and accounts. Most companies have a non-compete agreement or similar clause in your employment contract that prevents you from taking your 'book of business' with you. Even worse, this clause may limit you from even talking to your former clients and prospects after you leave. Don't go into an agency counting on the ability to bring your clients with you to a new shop. Moving a book of business rarely happens. The majority of the time, the agency owns the book. And even when the agency may allow you to bring the book with you, you will find that some clients just don't come over. When a Producer changes agencies, the client may return the phone call of the other agent that has been calling or choose to say with the Producer's former agency because it is easier. Moving business is difficult. Don't count on all or any of your clients moving with you when changing agencies.

What no one ever tells you:

1. The sales cycle is long (so very long). You may be calling on a prospective client for 18-24 months (maybe longer) before you have moved over all their policies, earned the commissions and actually get paid for anything. It may take even longer for very large or complex accounts. Patience is truly a virtue.

2. You don't get paid right away. Many clients will be on a direct billing cycle with the carrier or on an installment plan. This can mean that months and months elapse before commissions are posted to the account and any revenue dollars become disbursed to you.

3. The work is not done when you "win" the account. The "win" is not just receiving the application or even the BOR (Broker of Record) designation. Your Service Team becomes vitally important once you have the commitment of the client. The execution of the placement is important. What comes your way can quickly go elsewhere if you fail to live up to the client's expectations.

4. It is much, much easier to keep the clients you have than it is to win new ones. Maintaining service standards and looking for opportunities to upsell and cross sell your client are the tactics that will maintain and grow your book. Those existing clients are great referral sources and references for your prospective clients. You worked hard to land your current clients, keep them happy.

The insurance industry can provide a great career for you and solid earnings potential. However, like with most things, you will get out of it what you put into it. Keep in mind that acquiring accounts is more about client service than anything else. Keep those clients happy and you will inevitably get more of them. Be ready to play the long game though.

Failure as a Producer is common. Why is it that so many Producers fail? In the upcoming pages, I will tell you why Producers fail and how you can beat the statistics and become one of the success stories.

Secret # 1 – Know who you are and what you do well.

When you stop chasing the wrong things you give the right things a chance to catch you.

"Great companies don't hire skilled people and motivate them, they hire already motivated people and inspire them."
- Simon Sinek

The quote above is from a great book called, "*Start With Why*" by Simon Sinek. Any sales professional needs to start by considering the reasons why a customer would choose you to do business with. What is your "why"? When I start the process to engage a new team, I build a business plan and organize my staff. It does not have to be very complicated. We start with a big white board and I go around the room and ask the team, "Why should clients do business with us?" It is interesting to hear what people say. Often, they will talk about the price of the product, the name of our firm, our reputation or our service. Dig deeper into this conversation and develop a mission statement around your purpose and the purpose of your team. It is vital to know why a client might choose our firm and make sure we are delivering what they want and need. The perception of your team is important because they will pursue actions or inaction that matches up with their perceived function.

Why are you in this business? Take a moment to understand and appreciate the decision to work in the insurance industry. Is this an accidental change in your career or a strategic and carefully thought out decision? Understand your "why". When you have a mission and a purpose about your chosen career, your dedication to the industry and your purpose will shine through in your interaction with clients. Ultimately, my "why" is to help others. I am a customer service person at heart and my determination to help others has directly influenced my decisions concerning every job I have accepted and every task I have undertaken. Even this project to write a manual explaining how to become a better Producer originates out of my desire to contribute to the success of others.

I have met many Producers who are unable to articulate why a client should do business with them as a person or with their company as a vendor or service provider. If the Producer is not able to clearly communicate how they and their company provide superior services and processes as compared to competitors, the customer is unlikely to see any benefit from working with either the Producer or their company. Before you call on that first prospect, before you build that first target list, take some time to evaluate the strengths of both you and your company. Knowing those strengths will help you manage your message and identify those prospects that will ultimately be the best fit for you and your organization.

The best Producers can articulate the strengths of their agency in a short statement. Their agency's strength may be in Workers Compensation cost reductions, or in Casualty insurance programs, or perhaps they are a regional leader in loss control and loss prevention. Whatever the message may be, the Producer needs to be able to explain it clearly and concisely as well as demonstrate the financial and business impact of the solution. There will be many opportunities to talk to prospective clients and circles of influence. When a circle of influence can easily remember, and tell others that the agency and the Producer have a top-quality program for small group employee benefits, opportunities for referrals and warm leads will commence.

It does not sound complicated but you will often run across Producers who have no clue what their company can deliver and they don't understand their own value proposition to the customer. These Producers are doomed to spend their entire career as generalists focusing on 'anything and everything'. This means they will prematurely cap out on their potential and may never reach that elusive $1,000,000 book of business. Do you understand the strengths of your agency or brokerage?

As you grow and develop your book of business, the concept of understanding your strengths will not disappear. You can apply this concept to individual account needs, particularly when you are targeting very large or complex accounts. You would not go whale hunting without the right harpoon and the act of targeting large or complex accounts should employ a similar strategy.

Concept:

On a macro level, the Producer needs to first understand their own agency and what the agency's greatest strengths or differentiators look like. When the Producer understands, and believes that their agency has a product or service that provides an advantage over local competition, then the Producer will more effectively sell this product to their customers.

In the restaurant industry, the wait staff or servers are normally required or at least strongly encouraged to try multiple items on the menu. The reason they do this is so the servers can offer a genuine, sincere recommendation to customers based on their own personal experience. It is much more convincing for a server to tell you that her favorite item on the desert menu is the apple cobbler when she can tell you that the warm, chewy crust has a touch of cinnamon and the ice cream on top helps the whole thing melt in your mouth. It makes a big difference when someone has a personal experience with a product.

The same is true with the insurance industry. A producer is far more likely to win the property account when they explain that the Account Manager had a claim only last week where the replacement cost coverage feature the agency negotiated at renewal enabled the client to recover over $50,000 more than they would have otherwise recovered. The careful attention of the service team saved the client a lot of money. Examples will be more impactful if they are real, sincere, and something you have witnessed or involve situations where you have been a part of the problem-solving process.

Product knowledge is important and so is an understanding of how your company delivers the various products and services that your clients will need. You need to know what the agency's work product looks like. Understand the proposal and presentation process. Use this to your advantage because you will be able to discuss expectations with clients as well as the process itself. If clients understand the process and know what to expect, you are far more likely to have a satisfied client at the end rather than someone who finds the whole experience opaque and a mystery.

On a micro level, Producers need to understand their own personal and professional interests. The type of company you are naturally drawn to or choose to learn about in your free time is likely to be the right niche or specialty for you. Some Producers are more interested in technology or healthcare companies and for others it may be financial companies or restaurants. Once you understand the strengths of your agency, then look at your own passions and interests. Look also at your existing connections. If you have a background in the real estate industry, you may be able to utilize those connections and network your way into some great real estate clients. It will be easier, more fun and you'll be better at chasing clients where you already have a passion for their business (or where you have an appetite for developing an interest in their industry).

Ideally, you should try to identify three to five of the greatest strengths of your agency. These can be strategic focus areas like construction accounts or hospitality. The strengths of the agency could be in a product line like Workers Compensation or Directors & Officers Liability. What are those three to five strengths? How does your agency deliver on those clients or products? What is the differentiating factor that makes the agency particularly strong in these areas?

Why it works:

It is easier to convince someone that you have the best car when you've driven the car and know its strengths. Discussing a client's business insurance needs is very similar. If you lack basic understanding of business or don't understand the product offerings and service model of your agency, your credibility as a salesperson will be diminished.

Business owners and insurance buyers are looking for a trusted advisor who can help them through a time consuming and often expensive part of their business process. No one really likes insurance regardless of what they say. Most clients would rather go sign loan documents at s bank than fill out insurance applications for their renewal. Insurance is a necessary evil. The least you can do is make it easy.

The other important component is that knowing who you are and what you do well will help you avoid picking up clients who will not be a good fit for your organization. If the strength of your company is Workers Compensation and you lack resources in Professional Liability, you would be poorly advised to target technology companies. Technology companies have a very low Workers Comp exposure because most employees probably work in an office and sit at a computer all day. Yet the Professional Liability exposure is significant. Professional Liability for a technology company might include software development, intellectual property ownership, installation and maintenance of technology equipment and cyber security issues. Don't take on clients that need services your firm will not do well. It is a recipe for disaster to stretch too far away from areas where you can excel. Understand the strengths of your firm and target customers who feed into that specialty. Your clients will be happier and your service teams will shine if the client is a good fit for the overall focus of the agency.

How to do it:

1. *Read your own press.* Your agency has a website and marketing materials. It sounds like a no-brainer but read the material that your company has produced

and look for areas where the agency has depth, expertise, and is already promoting these ideas via their own marketing efforts. In addition to being a valuable knowledge source, the existing marketing material produced by your company can help you with your own marketing campaigns when you begin prospecting. It will save you time and money to utilize existing documents, tools, presentations, and publications rather than building your own from scratch. Even if you update, customize or otherwise make changes to the existing documents, it will give you a head start by being able to utilize some of the basic information already provided by your company.

2. *Look at the book of business* (the existing clients). If you want to write banks as your clients and your agency does not have a single bank on the book of business, you may be at the wrong agency or you may be chasing the wrong niche. The existing client base will tell you a great deal about where the agency is successful and where they lack skill, resources, or expertise. You are also more likely to get referrals if you have multiple clients in a similar industry or niche.

3. *Talk to employees.* Take some time to talk with long-time employees about where the agency shines. Ask about big wins that have occurred over the past year or two. Recent wins will help you determine the current trends. Ask about accounts that have been lost in the last year. Are several of these accounts in a similar industry or were they lost over similar issues (i.e. servicing issues originating out of the same department).

4. *Analyze your interests and connections.* The agency needs to have the right expertise to manage the accounts that are produced. Individual producers must also analyze their own interests, areas of expertise, and connections. Someone with a heavy restaurant background may lack understanding of the healthcare industry and is unlikely to have a significant number of hospital connections. Look at your own background and the areas you have a genuine passion about or fascination with and turn those into your strengths. Align your interests with the strengths of the agency and allow that path to drive you to a niche or specialty.

Measurement and Accountability:

First, you must understand the concepts, coverages, or industries where your agency really excels. Take this information along with your own interests and connections to determine the best alignments. Build the tools that you need to have conversations with prospective clients. These tools may include one-page sell sheets or coverage overviews. You may want to develop a presentation document that outlines the strengths of your agency and perhaps lists some of your agency's marquee clients.

Success can be measured through the ease at which you deliver your message to a prospective client or a circle of influence. Practice concisely explaining who you are and what you do. In your comments, you should be able to clearly identify at least one of the strengths of your company and how that strength helps clients receive a better product or a better price.

Hold yourself accountable for knowing your message and developing your process.

It can be very tempting to become someone you're not in the face of a 'sure thing' but resist. You must remember that there are long term relationships that you are trying to develop. If you misrepresent your ability on something early, you face a real risk of disappointing the client down the road and disappointed clients find alternate representation.

Example:

Know who you are and what you do well. You can't fake passion. I started following the JOBS Act and the evolution of crowdfunding back in 2012. I researched different platforms and began to call on some of the platforms that interested me most. I set up the conversation by explaining my interest in the space and my curiosity about their business model. I asked for a little of their time to understand their business.

As we talked, I explained my business (insurance) and my approach to emerging companies in the crowdfunding/FinTech spectrum. I explained that I was passionate about the industry and understood the known and unknown challenges they were facing. The General Counsel of a crowdfunding company agreed to give me a chance even though they were already working with two other brokers. "Give me two weeks," I asked her, "to show you what we are doing in this segment. If you are not satisfied with our work product after two weeks, then you are welcome to take your business anywhere else you like".

Within two weeks, we'd accomplished more than her other two brokers had been able to achieve over a four-month period. I knew the industry, the issues, and our strengths as an agency. Because I knew what we could deliver, I felt confident making a bold statement. In the end, we delivered an outstanding program at a fair price. This organization remains my client to this day. Know what you can do well and be confident about your ability to deliver that value to your prospect.

Secret #2 - Riches are in the niches

Follow One Course Until Successful = FOCUS
– *Robert Kiyosaki*

"Idea minus execution is zero. Action is the key ingredient."
- TJ Hale

People like to work with those they connect with, often those who are like themselves. I frequently see Producers who are unable to zero in and focus on a strategy because they are afraid to develop a specialty. Somehow there is a perception that developing a specialty will limit the Producer and pigeon-hole the Producer into a segment where they can't succeed. A specialty does not limit you to fewer options, it allows you to offer a greater value and more personalized solution to key clients and prospects.

Developing a niche will make your prospects feel special and important. Having a niche will help you to understand the needs of your clients rather than peddling the same insurance products to everyone that you meet. Everyone likes to feel special. Clients want to believe that their trusted business advisors understand their business needs on more than a surface level. Those who are a jack of all trades but a master of none will have limitations in their ability to develop trust with clients. If you are not perceived as a trusted advisor, you will miss out on the opportunity to offer a differentiated solution. Don't be just another vendor.

If you are following the concepts in this book, then you have already determined what your company does well and what industries or exposures fall within your own personal interests. Now is the time to take that knowledge and information and develop it into a targeted focus, a niche. In its simplest terms, a niche is just a distinct segment of the market. Most clients prefer to work with a specialist who understands their specific industry rather than a generalist who lacks depth in any area.

Having a niche or targeted focus in a market segment will help you in your discussions with both prospective clients and important circles of influence as well as make it much more likely that these conversations will lead to referrals. It is easier for someone to refer business to you as a specialist rather than as a generalist. Developing a focus will enable you to more strategically target prospective clients. Furthermore, during your presentations you will be able to more effectively discuss the issues surrounding their need for insurance products. Developing a niche is about getting laser focused on what you can do and what clients will best fit within your model. Laser focus gets results.

When you have an industry or group of companies that you can get passionate about, you can become involved in trade associations and networking groups devoted to this area. By participating in these groups, you show interest, develop expertise, meet decision makers and ultimately establish credibility. It is this kind of involvement that will generate referrals for you down the road and help you grow your business more effectively and with less effort.

Concept:

Developing a niche allows you be an expert or specialist in an area. Specialists can produce a higher quality result. Think about the difference between a restaurant with a gigantic menu that doesn't know if it's an Italian or Mexican restaurant. How do you know when you want to go there? How do you describe the restaurant to someone else? "Gee, I went to this great completely generic restaurant yesterday that had no specific focus of any type." Do you think that they will have the best of anything?

Contrast the generalist restaurant that serves everything with a restaurant that focuses exclusively on sandwiches. If they are focused exclusively on sandwiches, then they can spend all their energy on making the best possible sandwiches. They will be more efficient about their ingredients because they only make sandwiches. They can target their advertising to sandwich eaters and the times of day that sandwich eaters normally eat sandwiches.   The focus allows them to get reviewed as the best sandwich shop in the city. Focusing on a specialty allows the restaurant to generate a top-quality product because they are laser focused on a single mission.

Having a niche allows for targeted marketing, understanding of the market and efficient delivery. Working within a niche really provides an advantage when communicating with your trusted business partners and circles of influence.   Your network will be better able to refer clients to you because they can explain that you are the very best, a specialist in your area. Which do you think is more enticing to the restaurant owner? "My agent sells insurance" or "My agent is an expert in the challenges associated with food service issues like foodborne illness. In fact, my agent helps clients protect their financial future by making sure the insurance purchase is customized to restaurant exposures. Forcing your network to provide you with a generic recommendation such as 'my agent sells insurance' will be limiting. Your referral sources will welcome the opportunity to sell your specialty. Any sales process will benefit from having a strategic focus.

Developing a strategic focus or niche involves narrowing down the various types of clients or specialties to about three key areas. Some Producers are successful with a broader focus but for purposes of developing a million-dollar book of business, try to keep your focus to no more than three areas of practice. These could include Healthcare, Real Estate, Energy, Technology, or others. You get the picture. Think about what industries you know well and determine which of these industry sectors best fit the existing strengths of your agency. Look at where you have a natural interest or existing connections. As your book grows, determine where you are finding success with your industry focus and drop any sector where you have not developed any meaningful clients.

Why it works:

Having a specialty works because specialization gives you credibility and depth of knowledge that a generalist just won't have. For example, if your niche is in Healthcare, you have the opportunity to spend more of your time focusing on healthcare related issues. You can follow healthcare related claims and be aware of the specific issues or exposures that your healthcare related clients will have. You will learn the common questions that healthcare organizations ask which are different from other industries such as construction or transportation.

It is important that you take the time to learn about your niche. Saying you are a specialist in healthcare will only get you so far. You need to have the discipline to learn about the issues and exposures of your niche. You will find that clients in the same industry ask a lot of the same questions and have many of the same concerns. Networking and prospecting within your niche will make you more efficient because you will learn the solutions to the most common issues and questions.

In the marketing and prospecting process, having a niche or a specialty allows you to develop a more targeted marketing campaign and to be relevant to your prospective clients. Business owners receive lots of e-mail and solicitation calls. The way to get your call through or to get your article or e-mail read is to be relevant. You can be relevant by being involved in their industry and understand the issues your prospective clients face. Without some level of targeted focus, you run the risk of being that generic generalist. Who wants to be generic?

How to do it:

When you are trying to grow your book of business, having a specialty will improve your marketing results by helping you focus. If your specialty is restaurants, you can target your marketing e-mails with articles that are specific to the restaurant industry. Within any specialty, there are various subspecialties that you can use to laser focus on a group of prospective clients in a way that will make them feel like you understand their business far better than other agents and brokers.   For example, within the restaurant focus, sub-specialties could include quick service, table service, fine dining, diners, and food trucks. You can see that the needs of a food truck may vary somewhat from the needs of a fine dining restaurant.   However, since both are related to food service and have some similar exposures, you can build on your list of prospects by developing specific marketing campaigns for each subspecialty. You can further expand the specialty to related contacts like food manufacturers and distributors. The important component of this concept is to find the hub of your specialty and then start expanding to the various spokes.

Developing a niche involves the following steps:

1. *Isolate your target.* – Take what you learned from analyzing the strengths of your agency and yourself and identify two or three industry segments or groups that you can focus your efforts upon. Think about large categories like Healthcare or Technology. We will drill down to more specific sub-segments within your marketing efforts. Confirm that your agency has the right resources to serve these clients.

2. *Develop your message.* – What is it that you can bring to this specialty? Again, look back at the strengths of your agency and develop your message on how your agency and you as a Producer can provide the resources necessary to your niche.

3. *Tools of the trade.* – Look at the available marketing material that your agency has. What do you need to develop for your target customer?   Are there deliverables, marketing sheets, market connections or other resources that need to be created? Conduct

some research on the industry. Search for claims and other widely reported issues in the media. Use this information to determine the needs of the industry and further refine your message.

4. *Relevance is rewarded.* – Begin targeting your list of prospective clients with your refined message. Use these opportunities to talk about issues that are timely and relevant to the needs of your prospective clients. You can send out articles or commentary about current events, claims, or coverage features that are specific to the industry or category. Keep the marketing efforts concise, pertinent, and frequent enough so that the prospects remember who you are. Often winning an account comes down to providing the right information at the right time.

Measurement and Accountability:

Success from a marketing campaign can be measured in terms of first appointments or in terms of closed opportunities. There must be a certain balance to the quantification of the results. It is possible to have a wildly successful marketing campaign yet you fail miserably when you get in the door. You need to be able to analyze your process and determine if the failure occurred because you targeted the wrong accounts or because your sales presentation lacked the appropriate focus. Even worse, did you fail to close the sale because you lacked follow up with the client?

Each marketing campaign should be monitored for its effectiveness and the return on the investment made. An investment includes both time and money. Be mindful of the time you have invested in a prospect or niche. If the hours you are spending don't result in some successful placements, then perhaps you are not spending your time wisely.

Look at the target metric for your agency regarding the ROI (return on investment) for your marketing and expense dollars. This investment structure includes expenditures such as taking a prospective client out to lunch or a hockey game and more traditional marketing dollar outlays like sending out a mailer or placing an advertisement in a magazine. Analyzing the return on the investment dollar is not complicated. Simply take the amount spent and divide it by the revenue earned on the placement. If you are regularly spending more than your company's target metric in acquisition costs, then you are spending too much money to acquire clients and it's not working. Keep in mind that travel expenses should be considered as well when measuring the ROI on your investment into a client. If you are traveling across the country and spending time in hotels for a company that only generates $5,000 in revenue for your agency, the account is not going to be profitable or sustainable. We must remember that the goal of the agency is not simply to grow 'top line' revenue (gross commissions) but to develop and retain profitable business. Sustainability only happens when the clients are profitable to the agency after all expenses are considered.

When calculating ROI on expenses, the percentage used by your company matters considerably. Perhaps they will share this with you or perhaps they won't. Even if they don't give you a firm number, maybe you will get an estimate. Most will be well below 5% revenue to expenses. Some companies charge expenses directly to the Producer, effectively treating the Producer like an independent contractor. This approach can really keep Producers accountable to their spending but may backfire as some Producers will be too conservative. Others pay all Producer expenses out of a pool of money or from the overall budget of the organization. I have seen successful firms that have used low numbers like 1.5%-2% as their target percentage. A 2% percentage means that less than $2.00 is spent in expenses for every $100 in revenue. For an account that generates $10,000 for the agency, you should spend no more than $150-200 in acquisition costs. Acquisition costs would include expenses like lunches, dinners, travel expenses, promotional materials, tickets to sporting events, and all the other discretionary spending that could occur.

There really is no 'magic number' surrounding expenses as related to revenue. The concept that I want you to remember is that you really should be paying attention to how you are spending your money (and your time for that matter). I knew of a Producer that spent about 14% of his revenue on travel and entertainment costs for his client. Out of every $100,000 in revenue, he was spending $14,000 in travel and entertainment. Once you consider Producer compensation (20-45% in some agencies), agency overhead (15-20%), and support staff (35-45%), you quickly realize that there is not much left if Producers are overspending. Profitable business is the goal for both you and your agency.

Measurement is not just about tracking the dollars you spend in comparison to the dollars you make. Accountability is not about making a minimum number of phone calls every week either. In the next chapter, we will talk about what happens after the first appointment and after you have the client interested. Being accountable to yourself requires really following through on the concept of specialization and truly developing in the niche you have selected.

Example:

A Producer I worked with won the BOR on a leading outdoor industry retail account. This was his largest account with about $200,000 in annual revenue, a real whale. When he first met with the CFO, he shared his journal that chronicled all the hunting and fishing expeditions the Producer had engaged in. There were pictures, maps and stories. This was the Producer's way of showing the CFO that the account was personal, not just another client. The CFO said to him, "You're one of us." It took a few months, but finally the Producer was awarded the BOR letter.

Unfortunately, the work does not stop when the BOR is signed; sometimes the work is just beginning. Sure enough, two days later, the BOR was rescinded by the client. The CFO had signed a countermanding BOR and given the business back to the prior agent.

The Producer got on the first flight to the client's office and arranged to meet with the CFO the following day. He explained with all the available logic and reason the possible reasons why he had been awarded the business. He talked about his commitment to the industry, his understanding of the unique risks of the company and his value as a true partner of the company. Finally, he said bluntly to the CFO, "you're not making decisions like the CFO of a soon-to-be-public company."

Taken aback, the CFO finally agreed that the best thing to do was to award the business to the Producer. The Producer won the account back and kept the account until his retirement years later. Why did his blunt criticism of the CFO's decision win the account? What gave the Producer confidence to make such a bold statement to someone he had only known for a few months? The Producer was passionate about the client's business and spoke from the heart. The Producer believed that he truly could serve the client better than any other broker. The Producer shared his "why".

For the duration of the CFO's tenure, every time they saw each other, he said to the Producer, "Hiring you was the best decision I ever made." A client that believes that you have his best interests at heart will recognize and appreciate your efforts and forgive small errors in the learning curve.

Seek to be that best decision for a client.

Secret #3.1 - You just can't do it alone (Sales)

When a door closes, open it. That's how doors work

Alone we can do so little; together we can do so much.
— Helen Keller

The successful producer is not alone. It may be lonely at the top, but there is an entire team of people surrounding the producer that have enabled the successful management of the needs of the Producer's clients. A Producer that thinks it is possible to do this alone will fail. There is an important role for a Producer to play in the success of other producers. Finding a partner will make a big difference in your success.

Partnering with the right people will make a tremendous amount of difference in your success. When you join your agency, look for an opportunity to pair up with a senior Producer. You will learn a great deal from the partnership. If there is not a senior Producer that is interested in taking you under his or her wing, then look for a complimentary Producer in another area or in a similar specialty.

I joined a large agency at one point and was assigned a 'buddy'. My 'buddy' was of similar age and personality but worked in a different department. The concept was to make sure I had someone to connect with at the office and to ease my transition into the organization. Either it was that or they wanted a spy; I prefer to think it was to make my life easier. I would like to see more agencies pairing up new hires with an experienced employee because I think this would alleviate many of the stresses associated with being new to a company.

When I say, 'it takes a village', and that you can't do this alone, it's not only about managing down to the team that works on your accounts. No, you must realize also that quality mentorship will make a huge difference in your career. The most successful Producers I've ever worked with came in teams. Sometimes I think this team concept worked because there were additional lines of coverage being offered. For example, often I see a producer who specializes in Property and Casualty Insurance and partners with a Producer who specializes in the employee benefits (EB). This type of partnership is mutually beneficial. Since the producers operate in separate disciplines, they can be effective collaborators rather than competitors. As you develop the strategy to grow your book of business look at the other producers in your company and determine if there is an opportunity for a partnership with another producer.

While separate disciplines often will support a production team, two producers working within the same specialty that work together create a synergy that provides far reaching benefits for the individual Producers and the agency. For example, you could partner with another producer who is focused in the transportation sector and in this case jointly prospect opportunities or accounts. The joint prospecting process allows for the prospect of client to have multiple touch points. In your role as a producer you may find it very beneficial to be able to observe and learn from the presentation style and the sales strategies of another producer. The team approach can be incredibly profitable for both partners if both producers are committed to the partnership and effectively pull their weight.

How do you find a partner? Effective teams want to work together and have the personalities and common goals to successfully collaborate. A Senior Producer at your company may declare that he is too busy or refrain from taking on a protégé to avoid revenue sharing. If you have difficulty in securing the support of a senior Producer, partnering with another developing Producer can also be a good strategy. . The idea here is that two heads are better than one and working together as a team may lead to more successful outcomes relating to client acquisition efforts. There is value in having someone to bounce ideas off and provide feedback on presentation performance. A partner or mentor will increase your performance because you become accountable to each other. When you have a true partnership, each Producer fulfills their function and the partnership cannot function effectively if the other fails to contribute.

A successful Producer will also cultivate third party or outside relationships that can lead to referrals and recommendations. Sometimes these are called Circles of Influence (CoI) or Trusted Business Partners (TBP). The purpose of the CoI or TBP is to have a network of professionals that can assist a client with non-insurance matters and likewise for the CoI or TBP to have an insurance provider to which clients may be cross referred. When you are building your network of advisors and business partners, look for products or services that are useful to clients in your niche. When you can refer your client to a product or service that will, lower their business cost structure, improve their revenue, or otherwise assist in the growth and profitability of their business, your client will see you as something more than simply a vendor of a commodity. Seek to be a trusted advisor in their business. This means you must understand more about their business than just their insurance needs.

Concept:

There are two ways to build a production partnership:

The first option is to partner with a veteran, validated producer. Maybe there is someone in your agency nearing retirement that would like to take on a protégé. Perhaps there is a producer that has grown a significantly sized book and can no longer adequately service the smaller referrals he obtains. In cases like these, you may find it very worthwhile to share revenue on opportunities with a validated producer to obtain experience and benefit from referrals and references of the validated producer's book.

The second option is to partner with another associate producer or un-validated producer and co-produce accounts. This can work well with a producer in the same industry target group, such as healthcare, but a different line of business. An example of this is a Property & Casualty producer partnering with a producer in the Employee Benefits group. Another option is to have two producers both focused on a single area of practice that jointly prospect opportunities. Two can be more effective than one in this case.

Why it works:

The mentor / protégé model works because the associate producer gains valuable experience in real life client situations. This rapidly accelerates the learning curve. By watching how an experienced producer responds to client questions, develops solutions, and works with the service team, the associate producer makes fewer mistakes.

The co-production partnership works because two people working together will have opportunities to provide feedback and coaching to each other. There is something special about holding your peer accountable for preparation and expectations management. When there are two people at the table, one can listen while the other talks. The co-production model allows for greater observation of the client's questions, body language, and other non-verbal cues, while creating a more accurate mechanism to record the promises made. When it comes time to follow up with the client, the two producers can check in with each other to make sure nothing was missed and review the work product for accuracy and messaging.

How to do it:

Start by understanding the structure of your agency. Are there already processes in place to support a mentor/protégé connection or a co-production role. Think about how revenue might need to be shared and the potential conflicts that could occur.

1. *Identify your target.* Determine what kind of partnership will work best for you, your agency, your personality and your goals. The co-production role can be particularly lucrative if you have a class of producers that you connect with. The mentor/protégé relationship can seed you with some clients that you may otherwise struggle to obtain on your own.

2. *You'll never know if you don't ask.* Don't wait for the organization to team you up with a mentor. Identify the person you want to work with and make your move. This is not entirely unlike dating. Talk to the other producer and pitch how the partnership will be good for both of you.

3. *Do your part.* A successful team requires that both parties pull their own weight and contribute. Be mindful to be prepared, knowledgeable, and ready to work. Use the partnership to grow professionally by debriefing after each meeting. Learn from your successes and failures. Use your partner as a sounding board and a test client.

4. *Be in two places at once.* The partnership model can allow you to be at multiple events, meetings, or locations at the same time. When your producer partner is at a prospect meeting, you can be at a networking event. When your producer partner is presenting at an industry function, you can be proposing a renewal. Partnerships that work well enable each person to be greater together than they would be apart. Think about ways that you can maximize your reach.

Measurement and Accountability:

The results of your partnership will eventually show you if this is a successful strategy for you both. Hold each other accountable for lead generation and the follow up process.

It is important for each Producer partner to hold the other accountable for their contribution. Over time, an unbalanced relationship will fall apart. If you take time prior to the meeting to prepare and practice, your presentations will be better and more successful. Take time after each meeting to review the results and next steps. Pay attention to what went well and what could be done differently next time. You can review this information to adjust and correct for future meetings. Having a true partner that can provide practice and constructive feedback will make a big difference in your close ratio with your prospects.

Example:

One of the most successful production teams that I worked with focused on the private equity space. In this team, one producer was focused on the property casualty components and the other producer was focused on the employee benefits side. These two Producers split every account 50-50 regardless of who originated the opportunity. In most cases, they were jointly prospecting, however; there were cases where one producer had the lead or the opportunity and split the account with the other Producer even though there was no reason why they had to do this. This production team truly developed a specialty within their niche that became well-recognized within the geographic area in which we operated. In fact, in a single calendar year this team represented somewhere close to 30% of the new business that was written on my team. Their success was phenomenal. I want to emphasize that their sales success occurred although their gender suggested they might not be particularly successful in the discipline they selected. .

The other thing I observed with this production team was that their focus on building a team dynamic within the service aspect of the account management process transcended the production role. These Producers generated sufficient business to have a dedicated resource team that included account managers in both the property and casualty and the employee benefits departments. They held regular meetings of all team members bringing both the Property Casualty team and the Employee Benefits service team members together so that we all could holistically review the exposures and needs of the client. This approach reduced the problem that often occurs when one part of the service team is not up-to-date on the client requests or service issues that could be happening on the other side of the agency. It was on this team that I came to understand the exposures that many clients attributed to employee benefits. I also noticed how the property and casualty policies overlapped from time to time or even worse contained gaps in coverage that needed to be addressed. Had we not shared information as a functioning team, I know that many clients would not have obtained all the coverages that they needed.

The final benefit to this team strategy was that we all truly became accountable to one another. When we held regular meetings, it became painfully obvious if one member of the team was not meeting the expectations of the client and responding to all the service issues. Accountability often comes down to making those who are not contributing enough to the process painfully uncomfortable in those status meetings. One of the saddest days of my career was when the team broke up and our private equity business dribbled to eventual halt.

At another point in my career, I observed an agency that

strongly encouraged two producers to prospect on each and every account. The big advantage that I noticed to the agency from the dual producer strategy was that when one Producer left the agency there was a pre-existing relationship with another Producer. The continuity in the relationship with the agency made such a difference to the client. When a Producer left, this strategy seemed to help us retain accounts that otherwise would have been in jeopardy. I believe that both of the Producers in these relationships benefited from working together. In addition, the agency was rewarded with a higher rate of account retention. Again, I observed that these Producers, by working together in pairs, made better presentations and had better close ratios as well as a higher rate of account retention. They cross-sold more often and sold more product to their existing client base. The cross-sell success occurs in part because there is more than one producer focused on the client's needs. And when one Producer is talking, the other Producer is taking notes thus making the comments or requests of the client more likely to be acted upon. Nothing gets missed. While it may seem counterintuitive to partner and ultimately share revenue with another person, you are likely to find that a partnership is beneficial for you both.

Secret #3.2 - You just can't do it alone (Service)

It takes a village. Seriously, it does.

Success has many fathers but failure is an orphan. - Proverb

One of the most common mistakes I see is the failure of the Producer to make any meaningful connection to the Account Managers or Client Service Team. I find this wall between the two to be fascinating and very disappointing. The Producer cannot be successful without the confidence and support of the Account Management team. The Service Team will be responsible for delivering on all the promises and representations that the Producer makes in the sales process. It is important for all the individuals involved to feel like they are part of a cohesive team all striving for the same goal. The goal of the team is service to the client. Any failure in communication may result in poor execution and an unhappy client.

It's not just the Account Managers and the in-house Service Team that must be committed to the successful servicing of the client, but Producers need to have some understanding of the underwriting process, the underwriter relationships and the various structures that are in place to effect coverage and get a policy in force. I see Producers bully underwriters and force their Account Managers into "no win" situations that damage relationships. In many agencies, the Producer needs to step in on the marketing or negotiating process and helping to develop the best solutions for the client. The Account Manager may not be meeting with the client; thus, the

Producer must adequately convey the client's needs and make sure the solution will keep the promises that have been made.

Successful insurance professionals recognize the value in long term, mutually beneficial relationships. I believe most situations can be resolved with a win-win for both parties. At the end of the day, we want the client to win. If the client acquires the best coverage, the best program, and the best pricing we have achieved our goals. We need to be able to accomplish this goal while being fair and transparent with the underwriters and all wholesale partners. Any relationship needs to transcend a single deal. For long term relationships to be successful, we must recognize that we may need each other tomorrow or next week or next year. Burning out an underwriter to win on a single deal may be a terrible decision if that underwriter refuses to work on any other business for you, yet it happens all the time. Seek to build long lasting partnerships.

I believe we must prioritize the parties involved. The client must come first. Your carrier and wholesale partners need to come second. If you take care of both of those parties, your agency will always win. Above all else though, your service team must be first. As a Producer, when you take care of and respect your team, they will be motivated to produce exceptional results for your client. An unhappy team will do just the opposite. Treat your team with distain and they will do the same for your customers.

I took a job with a large, regional retail agency that was still majority owned by the family that had started it. I was on my very first appointment with the Chairman of the Board, who had run the company for nearly 40 years. In our walk, over to the client's office, I explained to him my service philosophy.

"Sir," I began, "I believe we must always do what is right for our client even if that means reducing a fee, taking a lower commission or putting so many hours into the project that we have exceeded our first year of revenue. If the client wins; we all win."

"Second, "I continued, "I believe that we must take care of our partners. These are our carriers, our wholesalers and our specific underwriters. We can't do deals if these people hate us. We need to be fair and think of our carriers and wholesalers as partners and not adversaries. We need long term relationships with these people."

"If we do these things, in this order, our agency will always win." What a relief I felt when he agreed with me. I was genuinely concerned that he might have an issue with my putting the agency on the bottom of the priority list. He told me that he had been able to build and expand his great agency by always putting the client and their interests ahead of everyone else's. That's why we win and that's how we win. Keep the focus on the client. When the client wins, we all win.

Concept:

If we are to be successful, we must have a strong team that is rowing in the same direction seeking to meet the needs of the client. Unless the Producer wants to fill out all the paperwork, negotiate their own quotes and type their own proposals, they need to figure out how to obtain the support and best efforts of their service team. The best Producers work well with their service teams to the point where they function as an extension of the Producer. The best service team is one that can anticipate the needs of the client and the approach of the Producer and bridge the gap between the two.

I have often struggled to understand service teams where there is no 'team' to speak of. I have seen agencies where all the Account Managers work in a pool and report to a single supervisor. These Account Managers may work on an account for Producer A, Producer B, and Producer C. Furthermore, a single Producer can find herself working with several different Account Managers in a single day. I think this setup is a recipe for failure. A team is a group of people working together toward a common goal. That goal should be to grow and retain clients. The real benefit of having a true team is that the team members hold each other accountable and back each other up in a seamless way.

The most successful agency I experienced used a team concept wrapped around a single Producer or specialty product. These teams would have an Account Manager and an administrative employee dedicated to a single Producer. Sometimes there would be more than one Producer working with a team but the reason this worked is because the Producer consistently worked with the same service group. The service team learned the strengths of the Producer and compensated in areas where the Producer did not possess a great strength. The team accomplished much more than teams at other agencies because they learned each other's working style, and created templates and work products they could share and reuse for efficiency. They covered for each other in a consistent way and the clients benefited from a broad perspective.

A newer Producer's book of business may be insufficient to support a full-service team. This does not mean that the Producer should be randomly assigned to multiple teams while the Producer gets started. If a newer Producer can learn to rely on a service team for consistency, the team can develop accountability to one another (i.e. the service team gets the quotes done on time and the Producer stops bringing in impossible tiny accounts with no understanding of the work involved in the placement).

Why it works:

Service Teams that lack confidence or respect in the Producer will not put forth the same quality of product or effort as those that have a functioning partnership. Account Managers and support teams will work much harder for the Producer if they are invested in the Producer's success. Account Managers and support teams that lack respect for their Producer will not provide the highest level of service.

Unfortunately, I have observed many agencies where the gap between Producers and Account Managers is a chasm that seems insurmountable. In many agencies, the Producers may earn more salary than Account Managers and this can create bitterness (why does he get paid more when he does not do any of the actual work?) With the high failure rate of Producers, often the Account Managers are just biding their time until the Producer fails and moves on to the next job. This leaves the few accounts produced for the Account Manager to try to retain without any relationship management. If you think Account Managers don't get frustrated and bitter about this orphaning of accounts, then you have not talked to any Account Managers.

Remember the 'team' for your accounts will also include underwriters and representatives on the carrier side. It is important to cultivate relationships here also. Seek out carriers that have a appetite for covering clients within your niche. Most of a Producer's time should be spent with prospective clients and networking to develop client referral networks, but don't discount the value of having a quality carrier relationship. I have received many referrals from a carrier that developed into profitable clients. The key here is to make sure you are nurturing all the members of your account service team. The underwriters are also a vital ingredient that will impact your success.

How to do it:

Building relationships will take time. First, understand the service team that you will rely on for your target clients. Get to know the team. Spend time talking about service standards, information they need to deliver a high-quality work product. Understand their preferred working styles. Talk about communication strategies and documentation. Engage in some role playing with your team to get familiar with the steps in the process and to determine where you need to be directly involved but also where you can back off and let your team deliver. The development of trust within the team will enable the Producer to spend more time working with prospective clients and executing on the marketing strategy and less time running down applications or gathering up underwriting information.

As the Producer, you are the leader of your team. As the leader, you must remain engaged in the process. If your team is running you off so they can wrap up the placement without you, they are trying to remove you from a critical part of the process. This should concern you. Your team should come together and engage with each other in pursuit of the common goal. Anything less is cause for alarm.

1. *Get to know your team.* If you were not assigned a service team, ask for one. If they tell you that you just work with whomever when you finally win an account, push back. Your team will make or break you as a new Producer. Don't leave this to chance. If your agency refuses to assign you to a team, go adopt one. Talk to different Account Managers and find one that is interested in helping you with your accounts so that you can build a partnership with that Account Manager.

2. *Feed and water the natives.* Take some time to make sure the Account Managers and service team members know who you are and that you appreciate their contribution. If they don't do their job, you will not be able to do yours. Say "hello" in the morning, participate in company social events, sign birthday cards and chip in for the occasional office gift. An Account Manager who believes you appreciate her will work far harder for you than one you ignore.

3. *Understand strengths and specialties.* You won't know who on the team has a decades long background in healthcare until you talk to them. If you do not get to know your service teams, you could miss out on the fact that a particular Account

Manager might know the CFO of the company you are chasing due to a working relationship that the Account manager had with the CFO while employed at her former agency. . As you talk with the service teams, ask about background, prior employment, areas of specialty, passion or experience. You may find that the Account Managers can help you significantly with the prospecting and closing of your new accounts. Don't take these people or their relationships for granted.

4. *Referrals come through many doors.* Your network of potential lead sources includes the Account Managers on your team and the underwriters that you work with on your accounts. While you don't want to badger these people incessantly (after all, calling on prospective clients is your job), it is important for these sources to understand your openness to opportunities. There can be valuable opportunities from an Account Manager that refers you to an account that she handled years ago, at a prior agency or an underwriter that receives a call from a prospective client who needs a policy but does not yet have an agent.

Measurement and Accountability:

A functional, healthy team will have open communication and a feedback loop. You can measure the performance of your team by watching the work product and observing your ability to meet deadlines and deliver on client requests.

Don't let a failure to communicate cost the agency money or clients.

Those that wish to be held accountable will ask questions seeking feedback even if the answer could have some criticism in it. Ask the team how things are going. Ask what you can do to help them. Ask what you can do better. Talk to them about the prospects you are targeting and obtain their perspective. You may be surprised that many Account Managers have great ideas about what might be most important to a client or prospect. Before you go out and promise a prospective client that you can cut their premium in half and add may extra coverage features, talk to your team and make sure that your objectives are realistic and that there is a strategy for execution.

After you ask all the questions, listen to the answers and find ways to update your strategies and make ongoing improvements to your processes.

Example

We had an opportunity to land a large non-profit account with the assistance of one of our Producers. There was a connection to the organization and through a friend-of-a-friend kind of referral, the Producer set up an initial meeting. The organization had a very sophisticated board member who asked some incredibly detailed and specific questions. Knowing there would be a great deal of nuance, the Producer called in additional team members to help with the initial client meetings, information gathering, and strategy development. By engaging additional team members, the Producer showed the strength and depth of our organization. When the client responded to the Producer after the 'pitch' meeting, they asked to only move a portion of their account because they wanted to work with one specific team member on specialty lines of coverage. The Producer explained that our team was all or nothing and if they wanted the specialty team, we needed to take a holistic approach to the entire account and would need to handle all the Property and Casualty lines. We successfully won the account at the meeting, became the BOR and then the real work began.

As we initiated the information gathering process, there was a learning curve as the team started working together. The expectations had not been adequately set forth at the beginning and there was a misunderstanding about who was filling what role. The marketing process went rather smoothly but the presentation of terms was inconsistent and disjointed. We had a great marketing result and we fulfilled our promise to improve their coverage significantly at the same or better pricing as provided by their previous broker. However, our team did not function efficiently. Our presentation was marginal at best, but we got the order anyway.

We executed on the order and the misalignment of the team did not improve. We bound the coverage but because the expectations were unclear, parts of the process were undone. Nearly 30 days later, we continued to await updated paperwork and applications. Our follow up process was far from efficient and the client had the perspective that we struggled on the execution side. After binding coverage, the client deserves to get their proof of coverage and copies of their policies in a timely manner. When the team is unclear on the expectations and their various roles, it is very difficult for the client to obtain the smooth, efficient result that they hope for.

While we won the account and we expect to retain the account, there are many parts of the process that would have gone better with a little planning. The   team's lack of experience working together caused a significant disconnect. Our team may have missed important coverage opportunities or made errors because we were so focused on trying to figure out who was going to issue the invoices and retyping proposal documents. Ultimately, we may lose the account because we made service errors. It disappoints me terribly to have done so many things well in the prospecting and sales process only fail on our delivery at the end. It is hard to win the confidence of a client. Be sure you can deliver on those promises and execute cleanly on the most important part, the delivery.

Secret #4 - Qualify and quantify - Prospecting Right

Proper Prospecting Produces Profits.

"I look at a hundred deals a day. I pick one." - Gordon Gekko

"Every battle is won before it's ever fought." - Sun Tzu

So often the sales process fails before it even begins.   To be successful in closing the sale, we must first make sure we are focused on opening the right doors. Once you know you have the right door, then you need to determine what to do when you get inside.   If you open the wrong door from the beginning, what you do inside will never be enough.

Before you even begin to build your prospect list or target list, you must be sure you have fully explored Secret #1 - Know who you are and what you do well.   For example, if your company really excels at claims management and you are passionate about healthcare, you may choose to cultivate vertical relationships in the healthcare industry.   Then, since you know Secret # 2 - Riches are in the niches, you may decide to focus specifically on hospitals.   By analyzing the strengths of your company and leveraging your own personal knowledge and passion you will be able to identify a narrow list of targeted prospects that are homogeneous enough for you to develop a similar process you can replicate and refine. Remember that developing a quality relationship with a client is not about your "pitch", it's about showing the prospect you are genuinely interested in helping their business. When you approach a prospective client as a business advisor and a partner rather than as a commodity vendor, your relationship is more secure and less vulnerable to sales pitches from your peers and competitors.

As a developing producer, you should focus on only two or three different targeted niche segments (no more than four). This can expand as you grow your network and expansion to logical related companies is the best approach. Many times, our production teams are encouraged to think big. Producers are asked to find the largest potential group of clients they can and engage in massive marketing campaigns or cold calling. I will argue that you need to think small. Narrowing down your focus to a smaller target allows you to hit the target. Good quality prospecting is not about doing more, it's about being effective. If you try to do five things at once, you won't do any of them well. When you focus all your energy on a single task, a single target, and a single objective, you are able to perfect your strategy and succeed in your mission.

Continuing our example, let's presume one of your target industry focus classes is healthcare and the targeted niche is hospitals.

Once you have identified your target customer, the decision makers in the target companies and your message of how you can help, then you can develop your actual target list. Use the Book of Lists, Google, Hoovers, or other resources to identify every hospital within a 100-mile radius with more than 25 beds. As you develop your list, you can eliminate prospects that are too small, too large, owned by out of state companies or otherwise fail to meet all your criteria. Qualify the leads as you go along by refining and managing your list so you develop   quality prospects that would be a good fit for your agency and for your specific book of business.

With your targeted prospect list, now you can troll LinkedIn and various networking groups for connections to the decision makers at each organization. When you know (or think you know) who the decision maker is, it becomes much easier to focus your attention on establishing a connection to that specific person rather attempting to get a generic introduction to any random person in the company.

You have your target list. You have your message. You have your connection (or maybe you don't and you will be cold-calling these people). Now you can focus on making the calls, connections and meetings. You have a defined strategy on how to start the conversation. A strategic approach yields better results and can be replicated over and over as you target additional companies in similar industries with comparable exposures.

Concept:

A laser focus on narrow targets increases the opportunity for meaningful success. Focusing on the prospecting process will enable you to target the companies that will be the best fit for your agency as well as significant enough to meet any revenue minimums. Furthermore, staying focused will help you build out your target niche area which will lead to referrals and additional opportunities. These companies will have confidence in your ability as you offer examples of your experiences with similar companies.

When you have qualified the account before you even make the call, you increase the chance that your call will be productive and profitable to your agency. It is a waste of your time to cold-call companies that are too small or outside of your firm's areas of expertise. Take time in the beginning to make sure the client is a good fit for the agency before you make the first phone call. You can even use this qualification in your pitch to the client as you explain to them that you are selective when choosing the prospective clients you call upon and that you have already taken the time to confirm you have the resources and products that will benefit the prospective client.

Qualifying the client also allows you to build a list of ideal prospects that you can discuss with your networking groups and business partners. These discussions will make it more likely that you will be able to obtain warm leads that result in a continuing dialogue with the prospect. In your qualification process, you can engage in targeted research that will allow you to speak with clarity about the issues that most impact the client's business.

It is important to know you can walk away from an opportunity that is not the right fit. If ultimately the execution on the account is not going to be successful to you and the agency, then it may be an account you want to refer to a trusted source at another agency where the client may be better served. One of the keys to success while building your book of business is often knowing when to say no. You want to maintain a focus on your specialty so that you will be able to achieve extraordinary results. Working on anything and everything will not develop the niche client base that will help you succeed as a new Producer.

Why it works:

Product buyers for insurance are interested in working with people who understand their business. Try as we might, we can't be experts at everything. You can however, specialize and become an expert at one or two things. When you are laser focused on a few industries you know very well, you establish credibility with the client that does not exist when you present yourself as a generalist. A dabbler in all industries but master of none will find it harder and harder to move "up market" into larger and more complex placements. Most charismatic brokers find it somewhat uncomplicated to win over small business. The challenge for growth emerges when the business is large and complex. Unique needs require a specialist. However, if hospitals are your specialty this does not mean you must completely limit yourself and write only hospitals. If an animal food manufacturer opportunity arises, you may pursue the lead and write the account or you may choose to refer it to someone who specializes in animal food companies. Know the industries where you can add the most value.

How to do it:

Certainly, there are many books and articles that discuss how to grow a network and use it effectively. Entire books are written just on the topic of how to network. Networking is important but smart networking is what works. Knowing the right people is much more beneficial than just knowing lots of people. When you are building your network and developing referral sources, be aware of the kinds of businesses and accounts that will come to you via these sources. Leads groups promoted through local chambers of commerce could be beneficial for expanding your network but may not give you access to companies that meet your target client profile.

Make sure you do your homework. Take the time to write out a description of your target customer. Refine your telephone message, introductory e-mail, mailer or whatever marketing medium you decide to use. Make sure the message is not overly generic. The purpose of focusing on a niche and targeting a specific market is to make the approach more impactful. Your pitch should be highly focused and industry specific. You know the industries where your agency has expertise and you are trying to share this knowledge with your target companies.

You will have a significant impact on your target customer if you are able connect with them and show a genuine interest in their business model and needs. Refining your focus and developing your strategy is key here. If you have no genuine interest in your prospect's business or industry, it will be quite difficult to convince them otherwise.

Developing a quality prospect list will take a few steps:

1. *Throw a net.* - Research companies in your target focus area. Your goal is to determine whether there is an adequate amount of business in your specialty to justify the focus. Look at publications such as a local business Journal which may have a Book of Lists or other similar resources to help you identify the various players in your industry segment.
2. *Focus on the right fish*. - How large should the hospital be? How many beds or employees should the hospital have to meet your agency's minimum revenue threshold? What is a reasonable geographic

area for you to service? When you know how large a client is before you make the first call, you limit the amount of time you will waste chasing down opportunities that are just too small for your agency. Analyze the opportunity and make sure it meets the size requirement for your book of business.

3. *Decision makers make the decision*. - Identify the decision maker or buyer in the organization. Is the decision maker the CEO, CFO, Risk Manager, Insurance Coordinator, Controller, or Human Resources Director? Determine who you ultimately need to convince in order to win the opportunity. This exercise is about identifying the specific role more so than the human being in that role. You will ultimately use resources like LinkedIn to find ways to connect with the decision makers.

4. *Refine your message*. - How can the strengths of your company match up with the needs of the prospective client? What can you bring to the prospective client that is better, more effective, more efficient, customized, or more specialized for their unique exposures? Ask yourself, "How can I help this company?" If you can't answer that question, you are not ready to call on the organization.

5. *Be memorable*. – As you send out your marketing materials and make your phone calls, be memorable. Many of these decision makers get calls every day for one product or another. Most are probably getting a call a week about their insurance. Be personable, knowledgeable, and informative, but most of all be memorable. The client is more likely to do business

with you if you can find a way to connect professionally to their organization and their needs.

It is important you take the time to qualify your prospects before you make the phone call when possible. There is a plethora of information available online. Before you ever pick up the phone, you should know some very basic information about the company. If you are unable to find any information about the prospect, they are likely small or new. Small may be too small for you to concentrate your efforts on them (you must stay focused on 'profitable' businesses). New can often be a good thing because if the prospective client is an emerging growth or development stage company, it is unlikely that they have a twenty-year relationship with their current broker. These prospects can frequently be easier to target.

When you can talk with the prospective client, ask relevant questions and take extensive notes. In your qualification process, you should have a plan that covers what you would like to discuss and how you desire to manage the call. Look for opportunities to partner with the prospective client, work together and find a common bond. Perhaps you may be able to refer other solutions to the client that are unrelated to insurance such as legal or accounting services. .

Measurement and Accountability:

All your preparation is complete so now you are ready to execute on your plan. Make the calls. Pitch your message and see what works. Don't forget that the most important part of the sales call is the evaluation afterwards. What worked? Why? What went wrong? If you could do it all over, what would you change? What would you do now if you were the client? If you fail to take the opportunity to evaluate your performance after the call, you run the risk of continuing to make the same mistakes over and over again.

A Customer Relationship Management (CRM) system can be used to track contact/connection points with clients and prospects. Many CRM systems track success at each connection point. If you don't have a CRM, you can track contacts on a spreadsheet if necessary. A tracking system allows you to be objective about your success or failure. You can't measure what you don't track. This is not to say that any tracking process needs to be complex because it doesn't. What you are looking to track is as simple as the process that you used and the results achieved. A CRM system can also provide a reminder that will alert you to follow up in a timely manner for those opportunities that don't close after the first phone call (and most of them won't).

Track the number of connections and the response. Did you leave a message and receive a return phone call? Were you able to schedule a first appointment? The "prospecting" process is about getting your foot in the door and making the initial connection that gives you the opportunity to showcase the skills of your service team and the expertise of your organization.

Remember that landing a meeting with a prospective client is the primary goal in the beginning. At the meeting, you have the opportunity to explain why your agency is the right fit for the prospective client. You will be able to measure your initial success by tracking the number of calls compared to the number of meetings obtained. Track your results. You want to review the data and determine the effectiveness of your sales efforts. How many prospects become clients? Look closely at the factors that played a role in reaching each outcome. Learn from your results.

Additional Thoughts:

Once you establish a   book of business, you still need to stay focused on your target client. A great strategy is to analyze your client list on a semi-annual basis. Twice a year, run a book of business report (a list of all your clients and all their policies). Sort the list by revenue per client. Draw a line under the top 20% of clients (if you have 50 clients, your top 20% will be your ten largest clients). Add up the total revenue you generate from the top 20% of clients. Now add up the revenue you earn from the bottom 80% of clients. Look at the numbers and the difference between the two. What segment do you earn more money from?

If you are like most Producers, the top 20% of clients (those top 10 clients) probably generate more revenue that the next 40 clients on your list (the bottom 80%). When you analyze the actual numbers, you realize it takes a lot of time and energy to service the bottom 80% of your accounts yet the return on your investment is far lower. What do you want to spend your time chasing? It's almost as hard to win a $5,000 account as it is to win a $50,000 account.   Because the process is the same and a great deal of effort goes into both processes, wouldn't you rather land the $50,000 account?

By reviewing your book of business on an annual or semi-annual basis, you can strategically focus on your target client, your target customer, and your target revenue size. Look at the revenue of client number 10 (the last one above the 20% cut off line). This should be your target revenue number for future clients. If you stay focused on larger clients, you will grow with larger clients. The risk as you build your book is that you will spend so much time and energy on small, less profitable accounts that your service quality on the large profitable accounts will suffer. If you allow this to happen, your large accounts will walk away leaving you with tiny placements. Any Producer can 'write business'. You want to be a focused producer who targets profitable accounts that see value in your process and product and will be long- term loyal customers for your agency. These are the accounts you want to over service and respond to every issue in an expeditious and rigorous manner.

Example:

When focusing on your effort to be 'memorable', be sure to make it a positive memorable rather than a negative memorable. I worked with a Producer that occasionally bragged about how he had badgered a prospective client on the phone to the point that the prospective client hung up the phone. Harassing a prospect to the point where they hang up the phone is not your objective. Make sure you don't damage the reputation of your agency or eliminate the possibility of working with a prospect at a future date. The sales process is long. It is better to leave a prospective client with a positive impression of you and your agency. This positive impression may pay dividends to you in the future.

I spoke with a Producer one day about a prospect he called. He had set up an appointment for the following week and was very excited about the opportunity. We started talking about his strategy and it quickly became clear that this was the largest and most complex account he had ever targeted. In addition, I knew our book of business did not have any other similar clients. It would be difficult to provide a peer reference to this account when the client asked, "who do you work with that has similar needs/exposures as mine?". We were not going to have an answer to that question. This was a very large client, a whale so to speak, and we had the appointment. Now what?

As we started talking about strategy, we began with the first secret, "What do we do well?". Our agency had a strong practice group in Workers Compensation and the client had many employees that were likely to get injured from time to time so Workers Compensation seemed the place to start. We knew we needed to emphasize our greatest strength if we were going to have a chance.

Next, we discussed how to assemble the right team. We took great care in determining which team members were the most qualified and who could showcase the agency and connect with the target company. We were thinking small in the sense that we only wanted to discuss Workers Compensation in detail and explain that we had similar experts in other areas. We wanted to show that we were an inch long and a mile deep in each discipline. Furthermore, we looked closely at the industry and the publicly available information about losses related to Workers Compensation exposure to make sure we were addressing a need that they would legitimately be interested in exploring.

We did not win the account. In fact, we prospected poorly and spent a great deal of time and effort on a placement that was out of our area of expertise. While we had an outstanding Workers Compensation team, we had no peer clients and minimal experience with companies of this size. Our Producer had not worked on any account of similar size or similar exposure and did not really know how the client would ultimately make the decision about whether to purchase Workers Compensation Insurance from our agency. Also, the Producer did not understand complexity of the decision-making process for a multi-billion-dollar public company.

I was impressed with the Producer for his ability to get past the gate keeper and obtain the appointment. He engaged a high-quality team for the meeting and the team executed well. In this case, the client was just not a good fit for our agency or for the individual Producer. The client's industry fell outside of the Producer's defined specialty or niche so his knowledge level was not as robust as it needed to be for the size of the company we were targeting. He needed to win some smaller Workers Compensation accounts and build his confidence and knowledge base before he attempted to harpoon a whale.

Riches are in the Niches:

Female producers in the Property & Casualty space are rare. This is true even though women have made advancements in the workplace and now own around 31% of private companies (Source: National Association of Women Business Owners). Even with this statistic, it is unusual to find more than one or two female producers even in a large agency office.

Some time ago, I was working with a recently hired female Property & Casualty Producer and discussing her niche or specialty. We wanted to develop a marketing campaign. We realized that there were many women owned businesses in her area and that this could be a significant differentiating factor for her as she competed with other Producers. A woman owned business might appreciate the perspective of someone with a similar experience.

The producer jumped on the opportunity because women owned business are defined and registered in such a way that make them easy to track. This producer focused on her unique strength and used it to open doors. She quickly developed a targeted prospect list that gave her a big advantage over the competition.

Secret #5 - Follow up right, follow up often

"If you wait until you're ready, you'll never get started"

"Nothing in the world can take the place of persistence. Talent will not; nothing is more common than unsuccessful men with talent. Genius will not; unrewarded genius is almost a proverb. Education will not; the world is full of educated derelicts." – Calvin Coolidge

The most important secret and the hardest one to master is the follow up process. It does not matter how well you know yourself or the agency you represent if you don't follow through. It does not matter how succinctly you have identified a niche and executed on the specialty if you don't follow up with the prospects. It does not matter how great of a relationship you have built with your support team if you don't manage the relationship with the client. It does not matter how well you qualify your accounts and chase only those that are the most valuable or how well you define your top 20% if you can't return phone calls, drop reminders and fail to oversee relationships effectively. Do you see a trend here?

In fact, I believe you cannot be a successful producer of any size in any company if you have not mastered the follow up process. There probably should be a whole book written just on how to follow up. It's not complicated though; you need to know what you promised and do what you said you would do. And then, of course, you must do those things. The execution piece is such a challenge.

Your deal is only as secure as your last contact with the client. We recently had a great meeting with the CFO of a fast-growing company. I spoke with the Property & Casualty producer and the Employee Benefits producer immediately after the meeting and asked how they thought the meeting had gone.

"He took the BOR's, so this is done.", said the Property & Casualty producer.

"I think we have him", said the Employee Benefits producer.

The reality is that until the signed broker of record (BOR) letters come back from the CFO, the prospective client is still a prospect and not a client. (More than two weeks later, we did not have the BOR letters back from the prospective client. It took nearly three months to win the account after this meeting. It's not over until the paperwork is signed.) It is very possible you can have the best meeting in the history of the world but once the prospect walks out the door, things can change. We don't want to put undue pressure on clients to make immediate decisions. However, we need to be very careful about celebrating our success before the paperwork is signed.

Even when BOR letters are executed, the client can rescind and go back to their old broker. Don't take it for granted the client is yours until it's on the books. It is important Producers understand the steps in the process and maintain an open line of communication with the client so that the relationship with the client continues to progress in the interim.

Follow up is also important during the quotation process We frequently send out quotes to existing clients or new clients and the Producer fails to follow up with the client. It is not the job of the Account Manager to sell the deal for you. You need to call the client, answer questions about the quote or the proposal and ask for the business. Releasing the quote is not enough to close the sale with most clients. Offering a proposal is not enough to close the sale. The Producer needs to take an active role in selling the product to the client and cultivating the relationship. Many sales are lost because the Producer fails to finish strong. Why would you spend all your time and energy finding the client, gathering information, and proposing coverage if you refuse to ask them if they want the policy.

If you are particularly fortunate, you may get warm or even hot leads from time to time. I had the distinction of being the preferred referral broker for a carrier for a time. The carrier would occasionally get a call directly from a client. These leads were passed along to me. These were leads that could not wait a week or two; these were clients that wanted to get more information on the insurance product as soon as possible.

By calling a warm or hot lead immediately (at least the same day) you double the odds that you will close the lead. Take the information provided to you by the lead source. This may include the name of the company, product they are interested in purchasing, and any other information about the company, and do an internet search. With just the client name, you should be able to locate their website and understand some of their basic business needs. When you call the client back, you should already have a solution in mind and know what additional information you will need to begin to implement the solution.

Concept:

Good producers use a Client Relationship Management (CRM) system, Outlook, or some other product to keep track of when they last contacted a prospect or client and what was discussed. A CRM system can be configured to have reminders so that the producer is triggered to check in with the client after two weeks, six months or whatever designated time period is appropriate. Successful producers, million-dollar producers, use these systems to manage their follow up process so that no prospect falls through the cracks.

The most effective follow up technique for a prospective client is to share something with them that is relevant, useful, and timely. For example, if your client is a hospital, a great follow up e-mail could include a recent article from the local newspaper describing a situation where a hospital had a significant insurance claim. A producer can forward this article along with some commentary about how an insurance product would have assisted with the loss. This kind of follow up will show the prospect that (1) you are thinking about them; (2) companies similar to theirs have challenges; and (3) you know how to address these challenges with insurance products, loss control solutions or other similar risk management strategies.

Following up is not just about closing a sale, it is also about building a relationship   Relationships take time. Our business is not about a quickie one and done sale. A CEO, CFO or Risk Manager is looking for someone to trust with the financial future of their company. Trust takes time. An executive decision maker at a large company is not going to award you the business the first time you meet with them. And if they do, you should consider not taking it because you are likely to lose the business as easily as you have just won it. Build relationships by finding common ground and reasons to connect. The relationship component is one reason the sales cycle is so long.

Why it works:

For follow up to be effective it must be timely and relevant to the prospect. When you can remind a prospect from time to time that you are knowledgeable about products and services they need, they are far more likely to engage you when their current representation makes a mistake or a new opportunity arises.

Effective follow up works because it establishes to the client you have the solutions they need. Sometimes these solutions are not immediately apparent. It may take time for the prospective client to understand what you can bring to the table and how your representation would be different from their current representation. There may be changes at the prospective client's company that could create additional opportunities for you in the future. Keeping up with the prospective client from time to time will keep you at the top of their mind when a need arises.

The follow up process includes communicating with the client when you have proposed a product or policy. The phone call or meeting with the client is vital to cementing the relationship and actually generating some revenue for your effort. Don't rely on your Account Manager to do this part for you. This is your client. Be sure to take ownership of the relationship. Your Account Manager probably does not see any increase or decrease in her compensation whether or not you win the deal.

How to do it:

Effective follow up is not calling once a week to try to schedule another meeting. If the client is not returning your calls, you have burned them out already. Often, a prospective client will take your meeting out of curiosity rather than need or genuine interest. Effective follow up can move you from a side show to a legitimate provider of proven solutions. Be mindful of what you send and the message the follow up delivers. You want to sound knowledgeable, helpful, informed and informative. You don't want to come off as desperate or overzealous.

1. *Recap and Refocus* – At the end of your meeting, try to recap your conversation concisely and suggest a next step. After your meeting with the prospective client, send a follow up e-mail thanking them for their time, highlighting the top one or two issues from your meeting and finalizing or proposing another connection point.

2. *Show up and be relevant* – When you have the next connection point with the client, show up and be on time. This sounds like a no-brainer, but you might be surprised at how many Producers fail to make it to the next meeting, phone call or event. Just as important, be relevant in your connection. If you

have another meeting set with the prospective client, bring an article or discuss an event that shows your expertise or underscores something from your first meeting. For example, if you were talking to a healthcare client about cyber liability claims, bring an article or press release about a healthcare company with a recent data breach. Be prepared to discuss the relevance to your prospect's industry and business as well as how you would approach a solution.

3. *Patience and persistence are both important* – Sometimes clients just don't need you right now. There is something to be said about waiting in the wings for their current broker to make a mistake or for the client to need a second opinion or an additional resource. Don't push so hard they push you away. Be patient because the insurance sales process can take a very long time. However, don't give up and don't go away. Depending on the size of the account, it may be appropriate to engage in a quarterly check in. Be relevant with the follow up. Send them an article that would be meaningful to the business or offer a recent success or example where you successfully helped a similar client.

4. *Ask for the business* – It seems cliché at this point to remind any sales professional of the need to ask for the business. However, your agency is still a sales organization and some sales truths are universal. There comes a point in the meeting or communication process where you need to check in with the client or prospect and see if a buying decision can be made. Simply ask them if they are ready to move forward with your quote or proposal.

If you are trying to win the account on BOR, ask if they are ready to engage you as their representation. If you don't ask, you may never get the sale that is staring you right in the face.

5. *Build a relationship* – And when all else fails, focus on building a relationship. In the beginning of a relationship you don't focus on the outcome. You are not talking about marriage on the first date. When you are building a relationship, you want to be looking for common ground and opportunities to connect. In a business sense, this may include volunteer boards or community activities. Maybe you want to learn about their business and share your industry knowledge. Find a way to connect with the person. Over time, this connection can lead to the business opportunity you seek or perhaps they can refer you into another account that would be a good fit for you.

Measurement and accountability:

The first things to measure with your follow up process are the relevance and timing of the follow up. Ideally, you should be making a touchpoint with a prospective client about once per quarter unless they have shown significant interest. Be careful not to send them the same information over and over.

Keep track of the number of contacts you have with a prospective client before they become a customer. When you track this data over time, you will realize that it may take five, ten, or more connection points before you are successful in converting the prospect into a client. Don't let this get you down. The sales cycle in commercial insurance is a long one. Once you land that client, they will be slow to move away from you also (let's hope).

Utilize your CRM system for the tracking of your success. See the References and Acknowledgements if you don't have a CRM system or hate yours and want something different. Watch your results on a regular basis, weekly is best. Track the progress and movement of prospective clients through the process.   When progress stalls, go back to the fundamentals and look for another way to approach your prospects.

You may find the same prospect needs a fresh idea to move them out of neutral or park. One of our producers was fishing for a whale of an account and was struggling to find the wedge issue that could get him to a sale. Remember, you may not win the whole account at once. For larger accounts, it is far more likely you will be given an opportunity to prove yourself perhaps on only one or two lines of the company's entire program.   The Producer went back to Secret #1 and looked closely at our agency and our team for what we were truly the very best at, better than anyone else. He looked carefully at the needs of the client using Secret #2 and honed in on the two areas where the client was experiencing most their losses and spending significant amounts on insurance.

The Producer took our top representative on Workers Compensation out to meet with the prospective client. Our agency performed particularly well in this area as our actuarial analysis on Workers Comp was second to none in our market area. Our representative did not disappoint as he proceeded to show the client how he could improve the overall process, save time, money, improve return to work times of injured employees and simply make the Risk Manager's job much easier than it currently was. The client was blown away. They were with one of the large, out of state national players and had never seen the kind of analysis we proposed. The client gave our Producer the opportunity to negotiate and place the Workers Compensation Insurance with the understanding that a continued strong performance would lead to additional opportunities.

My favorite part of the story is that the gate keeper at the agency told the Producer not to target the account. "It's too big," she said, "they'll never move." The Producer understood the strength of his agency. He understood his niche and how he could show value to the client. He understood the team and did not attempt to take this challenging account on all by himself. He did his research and knew that the account was large enough to justify some intense time and efforts and he was able to focus on the few areas where we could have the most immediate impact. He called until he got through to a decision maker and made sure to keep track of his promises so we could effectively deliver on the follow up. This was a newer Producer that easily could have followed the advice of the agency leadership and decided not to make that first phone call. As it stands, he could be able to validate from this one single account and never look back. Talk about a win!

Example:

I once worked with a Producer that I just adored. This Producer was a genuinely good guy and someone that had an unstoppable positive attitude towards everything he did. He was persistent and optimistic about every account. He had a hard time seeing that an account was never going to come over and because of this, he sometimes could not stop selling even when the outcome was obvious.

We had been on several meetings together and seemed to complement each other well. He had targeted a particularly large, complex media organization with some unique exposures. He possessed a secret weapon because the key decision maker was not a native English speaker and the Producer spoke the native language of the CFO. This turned out to be a key advantage when we were explaining certain concepts.

In advance of the meeting, we reviewed all their current policies and had compiled our list of errors, oversights, and things we would do differently. We were at the client's office with all of the decision makers, the P&C team, the Producer, and me. We spent the first part of the meeting reviewing our findings and it was obvious to everyone we could add value and we had some creative ideas that would save the company money. We spent the second part of the meeting talking about the transition process itself, the timeline for the renewal, the communication process, and other logistics.

The meeting dragged on. More than an hour and a half into the meeting, we could see that the others in the room (Controller, Risk Manager, and VP of Finance) were convinced we were the right team. The CFO struggled with any change and was having a hard time making a decision that would cause him more work in the short term as he would need to bring our new service team up to speed on various issues. I had watched this Producer in other meetings keep selling and fail to ask for a decision even though the buying signals were there. He kept talking to the CFO and then they broke off into a foreign language for part of their conversation.

Finally, the Producer leaned back just a little in his chair and he said to the CFO, "So, are we going to do this?" I was so proud of him. I had previously seen him walk away when the sale could have been closed. The CFO did not actually say anything. The others in the room nodded in agreement to move forward and the CFO finally nodded his head to concur. It was a great moment. The account generated more than $50,000 for the Producer and it was his biggest win of the year.

Sometimes you just must stick it out there and see if they are ready to go with you. If they say "no" then you retool and rework your presentation and live to fight another day. You may not realize they were ready to go with you until you ask.

BONUS – Excellence is in the execution.

Man who chases two rabbits catches neither. -Confucius

"However beautiful the strategy, you should occasionally look at the results" – Sir Winston Churchill

I have a colleague that reads a book a week. Most of the time, these books are read using audiobook formats while working out, riding on the train, or participating in some other activity that leads to passive participation in the book itself. And while I find this person very knowledgeable and interesting, I'll even use the term 'well-read', I also find this person to be unfocused in direction and ineffective in execution.

Knowing information is important but being able to put it to use and develop a profitable strategy based upon the information is much more important. I am, myself, a voracious reader of business books and articles on industry related topics. For better or for worse, my focus has been somewhat limited to those books and articles that I can apply to my daily work. In this way, my extensive reading benefits my working life.

Often, I find myself moving on from one interesting book to the next without really taking the time to apply the lessons I should be learning. I think most of us find reading is far more interesting than the actual doing.

The best book I have read recently was, *The ONE Thing; The Surprisingly Truth Behind Extraordinary Results* by Gary Keller. At the risk of spoiling the book for you, the concept is very simply, do one thing at a time. Mr. Keller suggests that you do the ONE thing that will make everything else that you do easier, faster, or unnecessary. This is really a simple concept.

Today, I ask you to find your ONE thing you can do so you can sell more and be a successful producer. Execution is the most important thing. Find the ONE thing you need to do and actually follow through.

Concept:

Knowing information and knowing how to use information are two different things. Those who are successful find ways to apply their knowledge to their situations and execute. It is important to learn from the experiences of others and from those who have found success.

Templates and worksheets can be fantastic tools to help speed up your sales process and create consistency in your execution. Starting over each time when the task is repetitive will take up valuable time that you could be using to refine other skills or prospecting additional opportunities.

Why it works:

Execution is the most important concept to appreciate in the insurance sales process. Even if you are doing the wrong things, with minor adjustments, you will find a way to be successful. Knowing all the right things to do will not be helpful to you if you don't do them.

There are not too many ways to say, 'Just do it.' Once you start taking steps along the road, you will eventually arrive at your destination. It may take a long time and you may have setbacks along the way. Taking the first step in the right direction is the single most relevant factor that determines if you will succeed or not.

How to do it:

Use the worksheets at the end of this book as a starting place or a guide.

Look for ways to streamline repetitive tasks by building templates and scripts. Although it seems like this might make your process less personal, your utilization of efficient delivery mechanisms will allow you to focus more on building the relationship and learning about the prospect's company rather than on trying to remember the necessary disclosures or formatting on yet another PowerPoint presentation. Focus on the things that matter but replicate and duplicate whenever possible.

1. *Build a map.* – Even if you know where you are going, a map will help you know where you are and track your progress
2. *Duplicate repetition.* – Any task that requires you to repeat steps, repeat tasks, or even repeat your message, is worthy of building a script and a template. It may seem disingenuous to have a script you will use when talking to a prospective client. However, consistency in messaging will save you time and improve your results.
3. *Time out.* – Set aside time on your calendar every day for planning and reflection. It seems like every

business book I have ever read offers similar advice. Planning your approach and reviewing your results are tremendously important to success. It is the constant refining of your process that creates consistent results.

4. *Don't do too much.* – Success as a Producer is not about doing a dozen different things. Success happens when you do one thing right consistently and then add another thing you do well. Focus on a single task, a single secret, and get it right before you expand your horizon. If you don't manage to make progress with the first step, how can you be ready to move on to the next?

Measurement and Accountability:

Reading this book will not make you successful. It is the execution of the ideas in this book, and in the many others you will read in your career, that will make the difference in your success.

Although it feels a little like a homework assignment, consider being truly active in your reading and research. When you actively read a book or a series of sales concepts, you are spending the time to absorb and process these concepts. A basic surface understanding is not going to propel you to the next level.

You can start the process of measuring your success by making notes of the top 3-5 concepts from the article or book you are reading. Stick to only the top concepts. When you have this distilled down to those top three to five concepts, zero in on the lesson and develop a strategy to generate a return on your investment of time. Reading business books, like taking a client to lunch, is about the return on the investment of the time you are spending. It may seem easy to listen to a book on tape twice a week but that won't make you a better businessperson until you bring those strategies into your daily business pursuits.

Example:

As part of my role with many of the companies I have worked for, I am asked to speak at industry events or other gatherings. Often, these events have many prospective clients in the audience and a sales partner or Producer will accompany me to the event.

On more than one occasion, I have been invited to participate in an event under the guise of assisting with the prospecting process for our production team. I spoke once at an industry specific trade show on a topic of interest to the audience. Our company had contributed money to have a booth at the event and there were local employees, a Producer and me in attendance.

At the appointed time, I rose and gave my presentation to the audience. It was well received and several attendees sought me out in the hours following my presentation. I had several conversations about the topic and gathered up business cards. Our booth gave away hundreds of dollars' worth of prizes in exchange for the collection of business cards. On the surface, this would have appeared to have been a successful event and a good use of time.

In the days and weeks following the event, it became clear we lacked a follow up or follow through plan. We possessed a huge stack of business cards and had presented a topic that was of great interest to the audience, yet we failed to generate a single new client from this event.

I have participated in enough of these events to now realize we must have a very specific, targeted, strategy for follow up before we commit to the event. Recently, I participated in a similar event where we did not have the list of attendees. This absence of information made it impossible to execute on a marketing strategy following the event.

A trade show can be a great opportunity to create or increase brand recognition and meet prospective clients. A trade show can also be a tremendous waste of time and money. Brand recognition alone will not make you a million-dollar Producer. There must be follow up and execution of the marketing strategy.

Steven Covey in his *Seven Habits of Highly Effective People* says that we should begin with the end in mind. Before you spend the time and money to participate in a trade show, send out materials for a marketing campaign, or even call a prospective client, think about the end game. How will you convert this time, this meeting, this prospect into a closed client? Until you can answer that question, you ought not to spend the time.

Tracking and Accountability – Did you sell anything today?

Remember, it takes years to be an overnight success.

"We are what we repeatedly do. Excellence, therefore, is not an act but a habit." – Aristotle

Any action that is worth doing takes time and energy. Follow through is the single most important characteristic to learn, perfect, and focus on every day. Even when the doors are properly opened and the pitch is good, the best deals fall apart when there is an absence of attention to the day-to-day details and the follow through fails. Know what you are promising and be sure to deliver.

You cannot manage what you don't measure. Your tracking mechanism will vary depending on your agency and the various software that is used. I find a few different methods are valuable in holding yourself accountable for the financial performance or production of your team or your book of business. Your tracking mechanism needs to have a few key components to it (again, you may use more than one system to cover these elements.):

1. *Prospect Tracking* – You will most likely track prospects via a CRM your company provides. This system has you input the various prospects and track the lifecycle of the client. This is where you would look at the total number of calls you made during the year and the result of your efforts.

2. *New Business Tracking*- You may be able to track new business in your Agency Management System, but most likely you will want to track new business on a spreadsheet or similar database.   What you are tracking is the new business you sold in the prior day, month, or year. Sold business is where you have the order or the BOR. Sold business is Booked when coverage is bound and invoiced. Some policies will be on installments or another billing method that could cause your results to not show up for some time.

3. *Book of Business Report* – Like a Balance Sheet, this is a snapshot of your business in time. You should be able to request a book of business report from someone in your agency on a somewhat regular basis. This report should show all the policies you have in force at one time. These reports are not fully reliable because policies may be in the renewal stage or the installments may show the premiums to be lower than expected. Also, some policies are subject to an audit or adjustment at the end of the policy period which could push the premium higher or lower. New Business should be tracked independently.   New Business tracking also allows you to make sure your new accounts were booked properly when they were entered into the system.

Accountability involves setting goals and working toward those goals. On the wall in my office, I have a mountain climber and a big cardboard mountain. At the top of the mountain is our goal for the year. Every month, I post a big yellow Post It Note with our current production and I move our little man up the mountain a little farther. You can see the mountain climber from the window looking into my office. We post our goal very visibly for a specific purpose. I want everyone on my team to know what our goal is. I also want everyone on our team to know what our progress has been toward reaching our goal. It is important to me to be accountable to each other in my organization. If we are exceeding our goal, we want people to stop and talk to us about it. If we are falling short of our goals, we know someone could stop and ask us about our progress.

It is hard to be accountable when no one knows what you are trying to do or how your progress is coming along. Don't be afraid to share your goals with others and to post them so others know what you are doing. You will find there is a little pressure to try harder to reach your goals if someone else knows. Talk about your objectives and your progress. Create some peer pressure to work a little harder and accomplish a little more.

Tracking results will take time and effort but it is effort well spent. Momentum has an effect when you can recognize the trending. When you can look at your results and see that you have won a new client every month for the last six months, you are just a little more motivated to make sure you follow the streak and keep on track by closing a new client in that seventh and eighth month and beyond.

Industry averages suggest only about 10-15% of commercial clients change their insurance broker in each year. Some estimates are lower than this. At a 10% attrition rate, you can expect to keep a new account for nine years – assuming you service the account well. If you win just one new client each month, your book will grow rapidly and you will be on your way to the million-dollar mark.

Stay focused on the goals of developing your specialty and building on the connections you have. If you can continue to expand your network of references, referral sources, partners and peers, you can grow your book without making the dreaded cold calls.

The first step to accountability as we have discussed in this book is to be accountable to yourself by executing on these strategies and concepts. You must take the time to execute on the ideas. Start today and analyze the strengths of your agency and your own personal strengths. Build an action plan so you can begin to track your progress and success. You read this far. Now take it to the next level and build a plan. Once you have the road map, success is just a matter of following the map.

I am a big fan of templates. When you can start with a very basic template to achieve a task you reduce the biggest factor that contributes to procrastination. A template or sample draft can kick-start your process by making the first step a little easier.

Be sure to check out the templates, sample drafts, and the checklists included in the Worksheets chapter.

Taking it to the Next Level

Once you have achieved a one-million-dollar book of business, are you going to stop there?

Perhaps now you are wondering, how do you build a $3,000,000, $5,000,000, or $20,000,000 book of business and sustain it over time. Developing into a multi-million-dollar producer requires refocusing your efforts on your book. Be very mindful of your strategy as you move forward into significant growth. I can assure you that no Producer with a $5,000,000 book of business has made it to that point by accident.

Ascending to the next level and becoming a multi-million-dollar producer requires refinement of many of the strategies in this book, specifically, Prospecting Right and Following Up. As you build a significant list of clients within an industry or niche, you will develop expertise and knowledge about a specific area. Often clients will ask for a list of representative clients in the same or similar industries. They may even ask for a formal letter of recommendation. These items provide some evidence you have the knowledge you say you have and can assist tremendously in enhancing your reputation.

Once you have a book of clients, you can refine your approach and target only on the larger and larger placements. It is a wise practice to evaluate your client list on a regular basis (annually) and scrutinize the distribution of your clients. You may find 80% of your revenue is generated from 20% of your clients. These companies at the top of your list are the kind you want more of. Look closely at the coverages you provide to those clients, and then return to the chapter on Prospecting.

As you prospect larger accounts, keep in mind you are more likely to be asked for references and representative clients from your book of business. Having a repository of happy clients will greatly assist you in building more happy clients. Keep your current customers satisfied and their needs met. Some of your best leads will be developed from referrals and references from your existing book of business.

Conclusion

Building a million-dollar book of business as an insurance producer is not magic and does not require years and years of training and specialized skills. However, it does require discipline and focus. If you follow the strategies outlined in this book to build your skills and hone your expertise, you too can develop the kind of client list that will pay you well. Your book of business is like an annuity on your future earnings. Believe that you can grow a profitable base of clients and add to it each year. Momentum is a wonderful thing. You just must get moving on those first few clients and be sure to analyze why you win or why you don't.

Follow the tools I have laid out in this book to understand your strengths, develop a message, build partnerships, prospect well, and follow through. No single skill will make you a million-dollar producer. Persistence in each of the five areas will help you to cultivate your clients and harvest the profits of a quality book of business. If I have not said it enough, execution is key. Great ideas are nothing without execution.

I wish you nothing but success as you develop your insurance Producer skills. Now go sell something.

Epilogue

2016 is a 'milestone' year for me. I turned 40. As the year began, I took an assessment of the things I wanted to accomplish for the year, personally and professionally. I realized (not for the first time) I had come a long way from my beginnings and I had been able to build a career and a life I was happy with and of which I was quite proud. I looked at my 'bucket list' and thought about how I had published some goofy newspapers as a kid and fancied myself a writer from time to time. In the past five years, I have been fortunate enough to publish articles in some highly-respected trade publications like American Agent & Broker, Westlaw, and even found myself interviewed by a Wall Street Journal reporter for an item in the paper. (I think I kept the voice mail from the reporter for at least six months because I thought it was so cool to have someone from the Wall Street Journal that wanted to talk to me.)

I get a lot of ideas about things I think I want to do but I often don't reach the end. After I start the research process, sometimes an idea is deemed too time consuming, too expensive to pursue or it turns out it's not something I wanted to do after all. Research is key for me. When I have determined there is a path, I examine the feasibility of following the steps and reaching the goal. I call it 'workshopping'. If you can see the path and ultimately the finish line, it becomes a lot less scary to take the first step of the race. When I sat down and really looked at the steps required to write and publish a book, I could see a path.

When I was an elementary school and junior high school aged kid, I used to think you really had made your mark on the world when you were mentioned in an encyclopedia. It's kind of silly, I know. Today, I am not sure anyone still uses an encyclopedia for anything so I think today the equivalent would be having a Wikipedia page. Perhaps the next best thing (or maybe the way to get a Wikipedia page) is to write an awesome book and become a well-known speaker on wicked cool topics. (I wouldn't mind having my own Wikipedia page – then I will know I have really 'made it'.)

This book is my effort to leave a legacy to the industry that has taken nearly half of my life and share what I have learned over my career with those who are trying to learn the insurance business. My experiences sitting in on meetings with prospective and existing clients has given me a unique perspective on the process. I felt it incumbent upon myself to look for ways to share my observations with those seeking to develop their sales skills. It seems like I spend a great deal of time talking to our less experienced production staff and even those who are experienced. My perspective seems to be very helpful to many as I can identify areas where small changes can result in big improvements in the close ratio. I want to be part of that web that connects everyone and the glue that makes them stick together.

I still have some things on my bucket list that I will be working on next. And now that I have come this far, I have confidence there is farther for me to go. We all need something to work toward, something that gets us out of bed in the morning and provides us motivation to do more, be more, have more. What's on your bucket list? Where do you want to go?

Thanks for listening (since this is a book you read 'listen' may not be the right word to use here). And thanks for making my dream come true by allowing me to finally publish the book I have been thinking about since I was ten years old. (At that point though, it wasn't business sales but this will have to do for now.) We all need a dream.

Please leave a review on Amazon or on whatever medium you used to obtain this book. Drop me a line via LinkedIn, Twitter, or other social media or visit my webpage at www.emergingrisks.net. Check out the Five Secrets / Sales Effectiveness link on the website.

Worksheets

"Plans are only good intentions unless they immediately degenerate into hard work" —Peter Drucker

Reading the stories and recommendations in this book is not enough. You must act on the steps I have proposed. The following pages of this book have a single page worksheet you can use to focus your efforts and execute on these strategies.

Know who you are and what you do well

1. What is the greatest strength of your agency?
2. In two sentences or less, why should clients do business with you and your agency?
3. Where does your agency have significant clients or market share you can expand upon?
4. What industries or businesses interest you most?
5. Where do you have existing industry connections or an interest in developing connections?

Riches are in the niches

1. Identify the two or three industry segments where your agency has a strength and where you have personal interest or connections.
2. What do you bring to this specialty?
3. What are two ways you and your agency provide for the needs of this industry niche?
4. Refine or develop marketing materials and communications (like emails) that are focused on your industry and what you bring to the specialty.
5. Generate a basic prospect list for your niche in your area. Is this a large enough, profitable enough niche for you to be successful?

You just can't do it alone

1. Who is your sales mentor? Name one way to connect and learn from this person each week.
2. How can you encourage and reward referrals and warm leads or introductions?
3. Name the top three people on your team. What roles do they play in your success?

Qualify & quantify – prospecting right

1. Identify and define your target prospect. What industry and geography is this company in? What is the size of this company? What are the related or complimentary industries that are similar in their insurance and risk management needs?
2. How will you qualify these opportunities? How small is too small? What are the key metrics you need to know (employee count, sales, etc.)? You need to be able to gather enough information to estimate the value of the account before you call on the prospective client.
3. Articulate the strengths of your agency specific to your target prospect. Write a script. What do you have to offer?

Follow up right, follow up often

1. Don't give your client the opportunity to forget about you. Check in from time to time with a relevant message.
2. Build a timeline and reminders for how often and when to follow up with prospective clients.
3. Be persistent but remember that this sales process takes time.
4. Ask the client to move forward. Failure to ask is asking to fail.

Excellence is in the Execution

1. Where have you identified time each day to plan and reflect?
2. Write scripts for introductory calls to prospects. Write sample e-mails for different industries, different topics. Look for ways to improve the consistency of your message so you can repeat what works.
3. Focus your attention on mastering one task at a time until it becomes second nature. Then focus on mastering the next task.

Tracking & accountability – did you sell anything today?

1. Review your results at least monthly. How many calls did you make? How many meetings did you have? How many proposals did you send? How many new policies/new clients did you win?
2. Watch your revenue. Make sure you are being properly compensated on the deals you write and look for opportunities to increase your value for each customer (what other policies do they have with another agent or what additional products do they need?)
3. Pull your client list at least twice per year (maybe even once per quarter). Ask yourself what other businesses are similar and would make good clients for you. Which clients might be able to refer you other opportunities? Who should you thank for being your customer?

For Further Reading

"I have no special talent; I am only passionately curious."–
Albert Einstein

Some of my most favorite or most influential books:

Blue Ocean Strategy: How to Create Uncontested Market Space and Make Competition Irrelevant– (2005), W. Chan Kim

Getting to Yes: Negotiating Agreement Without Giving In – (1991), Roger Fisher and William L. Ury

Raving Fans: A Revolutionary Approach to Customer Service– (1993), Ken Blanchard and Sheldon Bowles

Start With Why: How Great Leaders Inspire Everyone to Take Action – (2011), Simon Sinek

The ONE Thing: The Surprisingly Simple Truth Behind Extraordinary Results - (2013), Gary Keller and Jay Papasan.

The Starfish and the Spider– (2008) Ori Brafman and Rod A. Beckstrom

Women Don't Ask: Negotiation and the Gender Divide–(2007) Linda Babcock and Sara Laschever

Blogs and Internet Resources

Rob Ekern's Newsletter and Blog – www.crekern.com

References and Acknowledgements

Thanks to Amazon.com and Kindle for making the publishing process so much easier than it has ever been. CreateSpace and Fiverr are also great partners.

Special thanks to my amazing husband and wonderful kids for allowing me a little extra 'mommy time' to write this book and get it to market.

There were many articles, books and other publications that helped me with ideas and concepts and challenged my perception as I was writing this book.

Thanks to all my key editors, contributors and confidantes. I truly appreciate all of the support and assistance.

References:

Bronson, Caitlin. Agencies' hiring success rate is dismal: Industry Report. Insurance Business America. April 10, 2015. http://www.ibamag.com/news/agencies-hiring-success-rate-is-dismal-industry-report-20244.aspx

Nason, Lew. Why Do 95 Percent of Insurance Agents Ultimately Fail? ProducersWeb.com. May 23, 2011. http://www.producersweb.com/r/pwebmc/d/contentFocus/?pcID=e25a5b9c8bfd31781e35865a6521e69b